"Repression of conflict destroys countries, communities, organizations, relationships, and love. Unless we learn to use conflict to develop awareness, we will ultimately destroy our world. Dr. Mindell brilliantly and clearly teaches us how to follow the Tao of Conflict, the path of paradoxical awareness."

—Daniel Bowling, J.D.,
CEO, Duke Dispute Management Center
Durham, North Carolina

Other books by Arnold Mindell

Quantum Mind: The Edge Between Physics and Psychology

Sitting in the Fire: Large Group Transformation
Using Conflict and Diversity

The Shaman's Body: A New Shamanism for Transforming Health,
Relationships, and Community

The Leader as Martial Artist:
An Introduction to Deep Democracy

The Year I: Global Process Work with Planetary Tensions

Inner Dreambodywork: Working on Yourself Alone

Riding the Horse Backwards:
Process Work in Therapy and Practice

Coma, Key to Awakening:
Working with the Dreambody near Death

City Shadows: Psychological Interventions in Psychiatry

The Dreambody in Relationships

River's Way: The Process Science of the Dreambody

Working with the Dreaming Body

Dreambody: The Body's Role in Revealing the Self

Dreaming While Awake:
Techniques for 24-Hour Lucid Dreaming

The Dreammaker's Apprentice

THE
DEEP
DEMOCRACY
OF
OPEN FORUMS

Practical Steps to Conflict Prevention
and Resolution for the Family,
Workplace, and World

ARNOLD MINDELL, PH.D.

HAMPTON ROADS
PUBLISHING COMPANY, INC.

Cover design by Marjoram Productions
Cover art by IT STOCK INT'L/IndexStock
Imagery/Picturequest © 2002

Hampton Roads Publishing Company, Inc.
1125 Stoney Ridge Road
Charlottesville, VA 22902

434-296-2772
fax: 434-296-5096
e-mail: hrpc@hrpub.com
www.hrpub.com

If you are unable to order this book from your local
bookseller, you may order directly from the publisher.
Call 1-800-766-8009, toll-free.

Library of Congress Catalog Card Number: 2002103099

ISBN 1-57174-230-1

10 9 8 7 6 5 4 3 2 1

Printed on acid-free paper in the United States

Table of Contents

Preface

Democracy insists only that every person be represented. On the other hand, when we extend democracy with the idea of "deep democracy" to organize our interactions, networks, and the well-being of our communities and nations, each of us—not only the leaders or facilitators—deals with outer facts and problems, and also the subtlest feelings and dreams of everyone concerned (Mindell 1992, 1997).

For organizations, communities, and nations to succeed today and survive tomorrow, they must be deeply democratic—that is, everyone and every feeling must be represented. Deep democracy is awareness of the diversity of people, roles, and feelings, and a guesthouse attitude toward whatever comes to the door of one's attention. Positive organizational changes based on democracy's facts and figures do not work for long if we ignore our deepest feelings about the issues. In my earlier books on deep democracy, (or DD), I claim that future governments can only succeed with awareness of feelings and dreams. When we are asked to become aware of and value our deepest inner experiences, almost any group or world situation becomes immediately different, and manageable. Deep democracy is a crucial concept that can help shape the future.

While completing this book, I was pleasantly surprised to find articles in the U.S. news using the term and the ideas of "deep democracy" as I described in my 1992 book, *Leader as Martial Artist: An Introduction to Deep Democracy*. Little did I think, in 1992, that the DD concept would catch on so quickly or that U.S. Vice President Al Gore, first lady Hillary Clinton, or presidential candidate Ralph Nader, and others would consider deep democracy as part of their visions for the future.

However, visions of how to run organizations are far from being facts. To realize the vision of deep democracy, with its insistence on making inner experience an organizational issue, we must learn the details about how to use deep democracy to resolve organizational and government issues. Therefore, in this book, I look forward to sharing with you and describing

How to recognize and explore conflict, instead of conflicting with conflict and repressing it

Ways to enjoy and know your deepest self during group meetings

How to use inner experience in organizations

How to put deep democracy into practice when complex feelings and diversity issues are at stake

How to apply deep democracy to create "preventative medicine" in organization meetings such as Open Forums, in all sorts of communities, at any time, and especially during crisis periods

How to work with the surface issues that trouble our organizations, and explore the deepest feelings, dreams, and stories that create communities

How the mysterious background that hovers around each of us and our organizations contains the power of change

My burning passion in writing this book is to create groups and organizations where everyone *looks forward* to group processes, instead of fearing them. My personal agenda is that everyone in organizations will make a transition from being either a participant or a facilitator to what I call a "participant-facilitator." I would like all of us to enjoy playing the single role we have in the larger body, and in addition, I want us each to become one of its wise elders, in the role of the facilitator making group life easier for all. Anyone, in any position, be it low or high, is potentially such an elder!

Furthermore, it is my hope that organizations will get to know the mystical background that moves them. In fact, awareness of this background is a central organizational and social issue. I feel that social and practical problems cannot be well facilitated without access to the dreamlike atmosphere in the background.

Our organizations, communities, and world can be amazing places to live and work if each of us knows about the responsibility of using our own awareness as a participant-facilitator, acts as one who cares for the system's process, and sees its real and imaginary dimensions. Knowing these dimensions gives each of us more power than we realize; as participant-facilitators anyone can influence even the most intractable organization. Far from being disempowered individuals in the hands of powerful people and massive world machines, each of us has the ability to *stop* the cycles of history in which power moves from tyrants to the tyranny of the oppressed. In the terms of Carlos Castaneda's shaman teacher, Don Juan Matus, each of us has the power to "stop the world" (Castaneda 1972).

Process work is a wide-spectrum approach to working with human problems, based on awareness of signals and events occurring in the moment. Process workers attempt to follow inner experience and outer situations. "Process-oriented" is the attitude that the solutions to problems can be found in the process, that is, the flow of events and signals.

One of the distinguishing characteristics of process-oriented organizational work, and its application to group meetings such as Open Forums, is the special combination of inner and outer "awareness work." Process-oriented facilitation works with our inner lives and dreams, as well as with group life, and its dreams and stories. Process-work organizations around the world have tested and applied the DD methods I describe in this book in all sorts of organizations and Open Forums to improve the overall living and working atmosphere in communities, as well as in severe conflict zones in the world.

The methods described here are based on more than thirty years of experience with internationally diverse groups of people in the midst of multicultural, local, and international conflicts—in families, businesses, inner-city streets, and war zones. There are applications of this work to organizational development in small and large businesses, schools, churches, labor unions, military groups, and city problems including ethnic-conflict situations, mediation programs, community centers, neighborhood associations, and cooperative projects between associations. We recently used the methods of this book to deal with issues concerning an old concentration camp.

The histories of each organization, its life-and-death struggles, are abbreviated forms of world history. In and around our groups, subtle conflicts create and annihilate organizations. World history provides us with the outer, observable facts of conflict, which are the natural consequences of the behavior of small organizations. I don't like or completely trust statistics, but I do wish to consider one historical fact: Twenty-five million people have been killed while fighting in wars between 1945 and the present. In other words, an average of a half million a year, that is, more than a thousand people a day, die in war every day of the year.

It seems obvious that war is one of our most severe global problems and that democracy has not reduced the number of conflicts. In fact, although pyramidal structures of authority are breaking down worldwide, and self-organizing, cooperative networks of horizontal relationships are emerging, the resulting tensions have *not* diminished as a whole. In fact, they often seem to be accentuated.

The same holds true for organizations on a smaller level. People are hurt or "killed," so to speak, every day. As a consultant to organizations, I often observe that destructive conflicts could be avoided if people noticed them and dealt with group tension. However, the opposite is true: Most people avoid group tensions. In fact, the greatest world war may well be *conflict with conflict*. Why? In a way, it's simple.

Most of us are terrified of conflict. Although there are fewer political dictators and more democracy in the world today, tyrannical leaders still flourish everywhere, and most go unseen in every corner of even the "nicest" organizations. Such "dictators" can be found terrifying people in the most "democratic" organizations. Few of us seem to realize that while these tyrants might be the boss, they might also be just about anyone else in the organization—including ourselves. In fact, we or someone else can become terrifying, even while we are trying to save the day by insisting others be more egalitarian and conscious. Often such well-meaning, group "consciousness bringers" are unaware of how they push others about. Any one of us can unwittingly hurt others simply by being unaware of the powers we have and how we use them. If we are not careful, the very attempt to "raise consciousness" can simply recycle the very abusive behavior we hope to correct.

The book's chapters show how to notice signals, become aware of the roles we play in a given moment, and become fluid in communicating and dealing with role switching and in what I call "community dreaming." Without such awareness, we are likely to ignore our own behavior and the signals of others, thereby inadvertently supporting the abuse of power. Without awareness, we usually gossip about troublesome people instead of noticing and learning how to deal with organizational trouble. Perhaps we are afraid or don't really know what to tell them or how to advise them in improving their interpersonal skills. Or we run, shrinking our potential ability to change the situation, and are satisfied with retreating into the identity of a powerless participant who is the victim of her organization, dreaming of some heroic facilitator who will one day appear on her horse to save the situation.

Organizations often seem to be like families in which one or two nasty individuals dominate everyone else, while others watch in fear or look the other way. Since no one stops such unwittingly abusive individuals, they grow in strength, until the whole organization, or even society, must deal with them by imposing rules, laws, and worse.

My point is that considering the "dictators" or the system to be the problem is superficial. The deeper problem lies with the manner in which all of us do or do not use our awareness of the roles and "ghosts" (that is, third parties who are spoken about but not directly represented) in community. Each time we ignore our own hurtful signals and the signals of others, each time we ignore ghosts, *we* co-create a terrifying world, and destroy our own organizations.

Until now, most conflict work has been based on essentially logical procedures, good ideas, and above all, on our ordinary states of consciousness, where people are usually expected to be pleasant. That is why such conflict work is rarely successful in dealing with tension. Namely, we are rarely in ordinary states of consciousness when accusations and retaliation occur. Fear and anger abound. Heightened discipline and stronger enforcement of rules will never be enough to deal with the problems of our world. Conflict work without reference to altered states of consciousness is like a flu shot for someone in a manic or depressed state of consciousness.

In this book, I use a new paradigm for working in large groups, one based on *awareness of the flow of signals and events*. By focusing on the subtlest signals indicating the onset of emotions such as fear, anger, hopelessness, and other altered states of consciousness, even apparently impossible problems transform into enriching community experiences. I will share how everyone—people in schools and organizations, communities and governments—can use inner experiences, dreaming, and mysticism in conjunction with real methods of conflict management to produce lively, more sustainable, conscious communities.

I am thankful to those teenagers (who want to remain anonymous) and their parents who inadvertently got me started on this book. I am especially grateful to the Native American, Aboriginal Australian, African, African American, Asian, Hispanic, European, gay, and straight groups with whom I have worked and tested the ideas in this book. I am indebted to the process-work communities around the world for having tested many of the practices recommended in this book. I am also grateful to the small and large business organizations around the world for helping me apply this work to change such organizations into communities.

I want to thank Susan Kocen for transcribing the original notes from my class on the Open Forum at the Process Work Center in Portland, Oregon. For her support in editing this manuscript, thanks go to Margaret Ryan. I am also thankful to the following readers who greatly improved this work by giving me their insightful comments. (They are not responsible for its errors!) Thanks to Lane Arye, Tom Atlee, Midi Berry, Daniel Bowling, Jim Chamberlin, Hanna Chung, Julie Diamond, Ela Dieda, Jan Dworkin, Joe Goodbread, Kate Jobe, John Johnson, David Jones, Gene Hanson, J. J. Hendricks, Peter Irving, Robert King, Lukas Hohler, Ursula Hohler, Mary McAuley, Dawn Menken, Carl Mindell, Pearl Mindell, Ingrid Rose, Martha Sandbower, Heike Spoddeck, Wilma Jean Tucker, and Lily Vassiliou. Special thanks go to my editor at Hampton Roads, Richard Leviton.

My teammate in all community work, Amy Mindell, suffered, played, and helped me "sit in the fire" and work with more than one hundred thousand people worldwide, engaged in hundreds of community processes, organizational procedures, and disputes. This manuscript could not have been created without her. By joining me in this work, Amy has eased the pain of my search for a better world.

PART I

Conducting an Open Forum

CHAPTER 1

Beyond the Rules of Order

"We cannot dismantle one system
without having another in its place."
—Mahatma Gandhi (Sharp 1973)

To understand yourself, you need to explore your inner experiences. Likewise, if multileveled organizations want to know themselves, they need to explore Open Forums to understand their various parts. Open Forums in my definition are structured, person-to-person or cyber-space, democratic meetings, in which everyone feels represented. Furthermore, they are facilitated in a deeply democratic manner, which means the deepest feelings and dreams can also be expressed. In other words, the Open Forum is to a corporation or city as innerwork is to an individual. The analogy between the innerwork of an individual and an organization's Open Forum goes even further. Just as your personal learning depends on how open you are to your various parts, feelings, and dream figures, an organization's self-discovery process depends on openness to the diversity of its individual members, and the diversity of their inner and outer worlds.

Diversity awareness is multileveled: It is a matter of noticing cultures, ages, genders, races, sexual orientations, religions, economic backgrounds, jobs, abilities, and worldviews and dreams. Process-oriented work with organizations is based on awareness of and bringing forth the richness of our total diversity and complexity.

It is said of Gandhi that "he didn't want to win battles; he wanted to win hearts and minds" (Atlee; Bondurant 1965). The methods of the process-oriented Open Forum aim at doing exactly that. By fostering awareness of the deepest feelings and communication signals of *everyone* in the community, we can create nonviolent yet direct exchanges. The new procedures presented in the following chapters are adapted to working with organizations not as mechanical entities, but as *living systems,* be they schools, businesses, or cities.

It often seems to me as if the very people we have made responsible for leadership and global change are not always the best for the job. Most organizational and world leaders, activists, and politicians have little training in understanding people or helping groups to change. Yet most of us who are supposed to know most about personal transformation—namely, those in the helping professions—usually avoid organizational tasks and the problems of social transformation. The lack of conscious leadership is why troubled organizations turn against their troubles, and conflict with conflict. They assume that existing conflict is "wrong."

Process ideas are different. Instead of thinking in terms of the paradigm that condemns what's going on in a given conflict situation and implementing programs, methods, and procedures that implicitly look down on the people involved, process-oriented organizational work discovers the missing power of transformation in the tension itself and in people's behavior. In the new paradigm, *conflict itself is the fastest way to community.* Conflict is its own healing.

Democratic methods, rules, and laws alone do not create a sense of community. Rules and laws may govern mechanical systems, but not people. The new paradigm, which I describe in the following chapters, acknowledges that organizations are partially mechanical beings needing behavior change. However, in the new paradigm, organizations are also living organisms whose lifeblood is composed of feelings, beliefs, and dreams. Ignoring the flow of this "blood," that is, moment-to-moment experiences, disregards emotions and represses what I call "the dreaming background" to the everyday life of schools, businesses, and cities. Ignoring the dreaming background eventually depresses us. When "facts" become more important than feelings and dreams, we get bored, don't vote, won't go to meetings, avoid relationship problems, and become disinterested in public life. Disinterested participants erode organizations, precipitating their collapse as if they were empty, paper buildings.

In today's world, "good" ideas don't work without communication awareness. One side cannot truly win in a battle. In addition, one method alone cannot deal with human issues for long. In fact, our organizations are no longer localized in one spot; cyberspace changed all that! There are no longer simple localities in our second-millennium world. We are rather a planet of interconnections.

Therefore, creating deep democracy deals with community members not only as separate, local entities but also as sensitive, nonlocal interconnecting spirits of the times, which are constantly changing. In other words, each of our viewpoints has something global and eternal about it, for even if we are not around, there is always someone else who seems to fill in for us. In fact, any viewpoint is more like a ghost than a fact. Even when no single person represents that viewpoint, it sort of "spooks" us. We have all witnessed at one time or another how roles such as the "rebel" or the "unconscious leader" hover like spirits around groups.

Even in serious situations, process-oriented Open Forums can bring out the spirits in the background in a playful manner to reveal the community as a global, dreaming being in the midst of self-discovery. By taking the group's process as a teacher, everyone becomes a learner and leader, including young children and longtime gang leaders. According to William Ury in his excellent 1999 book, *Getting to Peace*, "In 10,000 schools in this country, kids as young as six or seven are learning peer mediation." He tells us that in the cities of the United States "gang leaders often become the best mediators, they command respect for the transformation they've gone through." The awareness methods of process-oriented Open Forums work in face-to-face interactions and on the Internet.

Using awareness in groups allows us to discover ourselves, the way we are. With awareness, we have access not only to our emotions, but also to detachment. Anyone who uses her awareness to enter the heart of conflict knows from personal experience that the emotions that arise are not always predictable. For example, I know from my own experience that the feelings involved in tense situations touch me deeply. Sometimes people scare me; they make me feel sad, or even removed from situations. If I use my awareness, I notice that sometimes my body shakes, as if I were in the presence of a huge monster, although the person I am facing seems to be acting timidly. Using awareness connects me to the excitement, the wildness and love in any given moment. Using awareness is a very different paradigm from using rules and power, because with awareness, the next step is not always predictable. Even monsters can be present.

Taoism: Ancient Chinese Paradigm for Process Work

To get along with change and survive the stress of conflict, we need some paradigm that is beyond those of danger and safety, war and peace, violence and nonviolence. These viewpoints are either *for* or *against* what is actually happening. If for any reason, you are against either conflict or peace, you tend to ignore anger and/or quietness in groups. Process-oriented facilitators do not use peace paradigms, which wage war against conflict. Process work is based on an ancient Chinese belief in nature called Taoism, which includes all possible states of mind such as conflict and peace, stagnation and breakthrough. The philosophy of Taoism is expressed in eighty-one sayings of the *Tao Teh Ching*. The various states of consciousness Taoism encompasses can be seen in the sixty-four chapter headings of the *I Ching*, or *The Book of Changes*. I understand Taoism to mean that we should notice and observe nature, then be at peace with what is happening, be it conflict or rest. If we stop fighting war and struggling against tension, we can give problems the chance to resolve themselves.

Taoism has been very helpful to me in working with small and large groups. My personal view of Taoism is, in a way, very simple. When I look around, I see that everything changes. Try to find one single thing on this Earth that does not change with time. Notice that there are no firm "things." The stars are in the process of transforming; the Earth evolves; everything is in the midst of flux. Each of us changes each day. This is the essential view of Taoism as well as modern theoretical physics. Everything is in the midst of change. Fixed things do not exist. In a way, everything is moving and dancing together.

The afternoon before I began work on this book, I went for a hike in the mountains and climbed for several hours into the hills until I stood on a high, rocky terrace. I looked toward the heavens and saw clouds streaming by, like blue-gray balls of cotton, flowing beneath a bright blue sky. Elk running across the meadows caught my attention as I gazed into the autumn valleys, painted red and gold by the changing seasons. Above were the clouds flowing across the sky; below, the elk running through the meadows. While enjoying this view, a thought came to me: the whole Earth is changing, shuddering, and shaking. The animals, plants, rocks, and stars of this universe are moving, not independently of one another, but together in a sort of dance. Just as the clouds, the elk, and the Earth dance together, so do all things dance together.

While I stood there perceiving this immense dance, I was moved to tears. This experience put the job of mediating organizational change into perspective as part of a larger, more awesome interaction—the world's dance. This view that things are changing and interconnected is the view of Taoism.

We could say that the way in which things move and change is a dance. Each dance is a kind of Tao. Conflict is that particular kind of Tao, that particular dance, in which you notice someone yelling: "You are stepping on my feet, get off my toe!" When no one listens, the dancers' Tao of conflict may turn to the Tao of violence. However, no Tao is inevitable. Awareness can change a painful situation into an enriching one. To prevent violence, we need to become aware of feelings and pain and of the call, "You are stepping on me!" In this moment, awareness can lead to new relationships, new dances.

This reminds me of a recent interaction my partner, Amy, and I saw in London, where we were working with a large group of people who had come from all over the world. At one moment, the peaceful atmosphere of the group was awakened by the cry of a woman bringing everyone's awareness to the pain of gays ostracized by their families and cultures. The group atmosphere, or Tao, changed; conflict was present. The very openness to tension introduced by the gays allowed those who had been repressing themselves to speak about their problems.

In one powerful interaction, Irish participants spoke about the ancient feeling of being "stepped on" by the English, and this opened the historical conflict between the Irish and English. At one moment, a sensitive Irish woman came forward and spoke of her sense of being less valuable in the eyes of the English. She cried, "Why colonize, why down us? Where are your feelings?"

An English man who had been silent until this moment explained that being a sailor in the English Navy had forced him to repress his feelings. The woman screamed in pain at him, accusing him of heartlessness. Immediately others surrounded the man to protect him from her. Amy and I suggested he be allowed to stand alone with her. The group parted and the two stood in the center as we tried to use awareness and follow their moment-to-moment experience. As always, we hoped their body signals and process itself would show us what to do.

Then, to the surprise of all, he broke down in tears, admitting with sadness that he had lost track of his feelings. To the even greater surprise of everyone, as he wept, she peered at him and suddenly exclaimed, "Why, you have lost your soul!" She explained that she realized for the first time that he was in a worse situation than she, even though she experienced him as the social oppressor. Totally changing her demeanor, she said she felt badly for him. To the amazement of everyone, they embraced, having reconciled their conflict, at least at that moment and in that city.

New Dances

In process work, awareness is the key. As in Taoism's view, the necessary next steps to relationships are found in the momentary situation. The job of conflict managers is not only to reorganize people, but also to help people recognize how their own communication signals and dreams, the hidden signals and feelings, the hidden Tao, so to speak, of a given situation reorganize organizations. These vital signals and dreams bring people back into step with one another. The point is to train our awareness to *notice* the necessary next steps *hidden* in what I will later define as "body signals" and "organizational ghosts." Awareness inevitably reveals the new steps that can transform even intractable conflict.

The Trouble with Democracy

One of the sources underlying the ubiquitous violence we are all increasingly concerned about is the governing democratic paradigm. Embedded in the foundation of democracy are wonderful ideals such as liberty and freedom. For example, in Articles 2 through 21 of the United Nations' Universal Declaration of Human Rights,[1] we find the right to freedom from racial and other forms of discrimination; the right to life, liberty, and the security of the person; freedom from slavery or involuntary servitude; freedom from torture and from cruel, inhuman, or degrading treatment or punishment. However, can democracy, as it is now formulated, really uphold these rights?

The root meaning of the word *democracy* is associated with power, not awareness. In Greek, *demo* means citizen and *kratie* means power. Democracy comes from the root words literally meaning citizen power. One of the original goals of democratic forms of government was to balance and distribute power; instead of only the ruling elite, everyone was supposed to have power. What could possibly be wrong with citizen power? If people could be reasonable instead of emotional, democracy—and the "good" use of power, might work. But without awareness of our capacity to interact, social power alone will never solve our interactional problems.

Inner Tyranny Instead of Democracy

There are two reasons why democracy does not work well. In the first place, democracy mainly addresses social issues, not inner, personal ones. Truly democratic human beings are that way only very briefly. I have never met even one person who is able to sustain an egalitarian, democratic form of consciousness toward self or others for more than moments. Without some form of awareness training, within the privacy of our inner autonomy, most of us behave like tyrants. When it comes to recognizing different aspects of ourselves, we become dictators who simply refuse to do so. If we are strong, we ignore our shyness. If we are harmonious, we repress and/or deny our anger.

Instead of enacting the democratic principle that the people or parts should all be represented, there is usually only one prevailing viewpoint—that of the everyday self. This "dictatorial" viewpoint makes sure that we do not listen to the various parts of ourselves, our feelings, longings, desires, fears, and powers. Democracy—which, in principle, strives to empower all the parts—cannot work as long as it is recognized only as a blueprint for external structures. To make democracy an inner experience, we need to engage in some form of innerwork or inner dialogue to create a deeper democracy.

Democracy's Power Problem

A second problem with democracy is that it is based on the concept of citizen *power*—more specifically, the power of the majority—instead of an *awareness* within each citizen. Perhaps in the best of all possible worlds, the majority is imagined to be interested in the minority's viewpoints. However, this is rarely the case. In fact, as Professor J. J. Hendricks of the Department of Politics and Public Administration at California State University, Stanislaus, points out, democracy without awareness is a form of tyranny.

Awareness is a more comprehensive guiding principle than power. By using awareness, we can track what happens to those people and parts of ourselves that are not part of the majority when the majority rules. Awareness tells us that the minority gets upset when it realizes that the majority is not interested in its needs and views and that the wishes of those with fewer votes will not be heard, even if they are supposed to be heard.

For example, if the majority of teenagers in a certain section of a city are of one particular race, sexual orientation, and economic class, and two new young adults of another race, sexual orientation, and economic class move into the area, they are likely to be ostracized. Democratic procedures, which provide guidelines for *behavior* but not for *awareness*, cannot forbid or even address the fact that the disdain of the majority humiliates the new kids.

Disdain turns to dislike, and dislike to marginalization. The outsiders must either leave or retaliate. In recent school shootings in the United States, retaliation was the choice. In one attempt to remedy an imbalance in power, the outsiders took their guns, killed thirteen teenagers, and finally killed themselves, effectively terrorizing the nation.

The details of the people and the city in which all this occurred are not the point. The point is that democracy is an outer form, not an inner one. The point is that democracy furthers power, not awareness. Therefore, no one intervenes when a person or group exerts its psychological power and "rules" others. Today's democracy is like an old dance. We need a new dance, a deeper democracy, based on awareness of what is happening inside ourselves and others.

Robert's Rules of Order

Before exploring the methods of creating a deeper democracy that can be used in meetings of all kinds, let us think about prevailing, standard, quasilegal democratic procedures in detail. One classic, cosmopolitan blueprint for such procedures that can be found in parliamentary methods in meetings everywhere in the United States and Canada is *Robert's Rules of Order*. In Switzerland, the analogous procedure is called the *Vereinsrecht*. Each country has its own name for such methods. Wherever meetings occur, something like *Robert's Rules of Order* appears, regardless of the organization or country.

The U.S. rules of order are related to Brigadier General Robert. Who was Robert? Henry Martyn Robert was a U.S. Army man who lived during the Civil War (in the United States). In an effort to bring order to chaotic meetings, Robert created his Rules of Order.[2] The rules streamlined the conduct of assemblies by creating linear proceedings geared toward accomplishing a given task. Today Robert's rules are widely used in the United States for all kinds of meetings, from church groups to the Congress. Even where the rules are not adhered to strin-gently, the spirit of orderliness implicit in these specifications is invoked, especially whenever chaos threatens or when groups must make decisions around contentious issues.

The rules clearly rank *order* above *emotions*. In fact, "uniformity of proceeding" was meant to prevent "capriciousness."[3] The rules value linearity above spontaneity, the known above the unpredictable. "Decency"—that is, conformity to mainstream standards of taste and propriety—is held above other standards of taste and propriety. In other words, Robert's conventions favor mainly the mainstream—which means in the U.S. white, Anglo-Saxon—cultural norms over other cultural norms.[4] In my experience, the kind of cul-tural rigidity found in Robert's rules is not limited to any one culture; everywhere that legal forms are used in organizations, mainstream ideas about power and orderliness are invoked to dominate feelings that do not fit.

You Are Out of Order!

There are obvious benefits to the rules; one of them is "regularity." However, what about people who are not the "regular" types? Robert did not address the effects of his rules on the individuals who are "restrained," judged so because they are "capricious." The rules unwit-tingly marginalize "irregular" people, feelings, and emotions while sup-porting the communication style of one culture over others. Furthermore, there is little awareness of nonmajority feelings, which are covertly forbidden or else simply ruled "out of order."

How would you feel if you were consistently silenced with the words, "Be quiet, you are out of order"? You would probably feel deval-ued, unhappy, perhaps shamed, or worse. If this silencing continued over long periods, a natural reaction would be depression, perhaps even drug abuse and suicide, or else anger, fury, rebellion, and revenge.

The spirit behind *Robert's Rules of Order* makes it impossible for cer-tain people to be heard. In a way, their choices are break the rules, sink into depression, or strike out in anger and retaliation. Perhaps that is one reason why our "correctional" psychiatric institutions are filled with "minority" people, those who have long been marginalized, depressed, and angry, to say the least. Mainstream parliamentary and business procedures unwittingly lead to the abuse of power in relation to the very minorities democratic procedures were supposed to treat as equals. Thus, Robert is a spirit ghost with two faces. One face benevolently enforces discipline and order, while the other ignores the "capriciousness" (that is, irrational and unpredictable behavior). The result is that two ghosts dominate every business, government, school, and group meeting; one ghost is Robert the Righteous, and the other ghost is Caprice the Saboteur.

So what's next? When Robert's rules are not enforced, people who are undesirable, overly emotional, and disorderly—as deemed by Robert—are bound to participate and "disturb" meetings. All one-sided procedures that favor rules over awareness and emotions (or emotions above rules) ignore, per force, at least half of human nature. So can we respect Robert and allow the forbidden spirit of Caprice to exist at the same time?

Deep Democracy

The philosophy of deep democracy claims that *all* people, parts, and feelings are needed. Deep democracy appreciates present democratic forms but adds to them the need for awareness of feelings and atmosphere in moment-to-moment interactions and institutional practices. Deep democracy uses linear, organizational rituals, rights, and fair procedures *after subtle, nonverbal experiences have been articulated and valued.*

Imagine the following situation, which is an abbreviated report of a conflict about land rights between Aboriginal people and non-Aboriginal government officials. (I have disguised any distinguishing details to protect the people involved.)

Amy and I were facilitating a gathering of hundreds of people focused on the use of their land. In the front of a packed room, a heated debate broke out when Aboriginal people tried to explain that they had always hunted in a given territory until these rights were denied them by the government. The government officials tried to describe their viewpoint: "We are simply doing our job; let's call for a vote on the situation."

Suddenly there was commotion from an Aboriginal group in the back of the room. A woman from that group emerged and walked proudly forward, facing the head government official. He told her she was "out of order" and that the moment had come for a vote. Still she stood in front of that official, quietly looking him straight in the eye. Everyone was silent. Then, with incredible pathos, she spoke—almost singing—about the suffering of her people, then broke into dance movements for a minute or two while everyone watched, spellbound.

When she caught her breath, she said voting would only create more depression and suicide among her people; she wanted to remind everyone of this tragedy. Then she shook convulsively from head to foot. Finally, catching her breath, she pleaded, "Let's work together." It was as if the Great Spirit had spoken through her.

She may have been "out of order" according to "Robert the Righteous," but according to "Caprice," she was right on target: her marginalized emotions broke the barriers separating the Aboriginal people from the government. A deep sense of community was created between diverse peoples, at least for that time and space. We all decided to work together instead of against one another and could then proceed in linear fashion to create new directions, to which all agreed and from which all could prosper.

The point of the story is that democratic procedures such as Robert's Rules of Order work best only when they have been *preceded* by awareness of the deepest inner experiences of the group's members. Democracy as an outer form has great value, but without precise awareness of inner states, it can unwittingly propagate abuse and denigration by supporting power over people. Deeper democracy requires educating ourselves to notice all our inner experiences while dealing with the outer world, holding an awareness in a given moment of feelings, dreaming, and social power.

Open Forum Training:
Leadership or Awareness?

I quoted Gandhi in the beginning of this chapter as saying, "We cannot dismantle one system without having another in its place." To put deep democracy in place, we need practice and training. To create the new system, I am going to assume that you, the reader

> want to facilitate relationships among people of all races, ages, and economic positions who have different viewpoints
>
> are interested in training your awareness to resolve tensions in yourself and among friends, family, business organizations, informal groups, and international political arenas

Training addresses your possible fears. It is okay to be uncertain about creating and facilitating groups or creating Open Forums. However, if you are consistently afraid of groups, perhaps you are either too ambitious and want to save everyone, or think that you must be managing the situations at hand.

In this case, it may be helpful to remember that if you want to do too much, you will have to depend on using your own power, and that dependence will exhaust you and make you uncertain. We do not need leaders who can change the world because of their personal power, because change is inherent in people and nature. Our communities, however, need our essential selves and our awareness, not our power, to notice and track such changes.

Our world needs our awareness of the roles, themes, and feelings we experience. Insecurity occurs if we push to succeed. Let nature help with the work. We do not need more of the standard kind of leaders, but instead are looking for sensitive facilitators with moment-to-moment awareness.

To prepare you to facilitate such Open Forums, I will employ recent research on the nature of group processes involving emotional dialogue, subtle aspects of power, and conflict management in both small and large groups. The conditions under which these variables have been studied include monolingual as well as multiethnic, multinational, public, and organizational situations involving topics from finance to war. I will be speaking from experience with on-the-spot training of individuals and small teams, dealing with Open Forums of up to several thousand people.

I personally hope more people will learn how to conduct Open Forums, not only in their organizations and cities, but in their families. Open Forums can contribute to improving the situation in your little world as well as in the world at large. It is one way of putting your "drop in the bucket." It is a way of becoming an elder and of discovering eldership in your communities. If you have any bit of an elder within yourself—that is, if you have learned anything from the hard knocks in your life, gained any wisdom and detachment about being a human being—then the Open Forum is a good place to share your awareness and your gifts and help others as well. This world of ours is not just run by governments, but by the wisdom and dreams of elders like yourself, people coming forward to coach others in developing awareness of world changes and "inalienable rights."

Ask your deepest self if it is interested in helping out, and if it is, then begin! Identify the main issue, then invite people from different sides of a community issue to speak at an Open Forum organized by you in your school, business, group, or town. The detailed methods and procedures from this book will help. If you want more information on process-oriented methods of helping organizations solve apparently intractable problems, see my *Year One* for an overview of conflict work. The *Leader as Martial Artist* gives you a general background to the methods, and my *Sitting in the Fire* addresses large-group work with highly emotional issues around war, race, and gender. A summary of methods can be found in the epilogue.

What to Expect in the Following Chapters

Part 1 discusses how to prepare for an open meeting; how to begin, conduct, and finally end an Open Forum; and how to create new ones. Part 2 discusses how to advance your personal development and group awareness skills.

PART I. CONDUCTING AN OPEN FORUM

Chapter 2, "The Open Forum as Outer and Innerwork," explores the history and meaning of town meetings and how they can heal organizational and global problems.

In chapter 3, "The Open Forum as Groupwork," I discuss how to advertise and get people to attend, whom to invite, and innerwork procedures to prepare yourself as a facilitator.

In chapters 4 and 5, "The Facilitator's Awareness Work" and "Consciousness during Attack," respectively, I study awareness procedures and skills needed to facilitate group processes and how to deal with attack.

Chapter 6, "Ending with Why You Began," explains how to complete a first Open Forum and how to prepare the group for what is coming next. If your group decides to have ongoing forums, which I hope it will, this chapter gives you tips on how to lead into them.

Part II. A SECOND REVOLUTION

In part 1, you will have learned basic methods of preparing, conducting, and ending an Open Forum. You will have learned awareness steps that are general enough to help you get through your first forum. However, as you develop and relax as a facilitator, your ability to notice more about what is happening increases. Part 2 deals with advanced awareness tips and shows how such awareness itself is a *second* revolution. (The *first* revolutions are about equal distribution of material privileges such as voting power, property, etc.)

Chapter 7, "The Psychosocial Activist," discusses typical roles, interaction patterns, and issues you can expect to meet in just about any meeting, anywhere in the world. In particular, I study Open Forums conducted in Asia, Australia, Europe, South America, and the United States. Dramatic learning scenes are described in this chapter.

In chapter 8, "The Dreaming Background to Community," I explore ways of facilitating in the face of global hopelessness about world change, and describe how to deal with extreme moments and near violence in Open Forums.

In chapter 9, "The Media as a Wake-Up Dream," the focus is on how to create and use the media—which is often more a bother than a help—for the benefit of your community.

Chapter 10, "The Flu Shot against War," speaks about what drives individuals and groups to violence and how to deal with these extreme states of consciousness for the benefit of all. Tackling the problem of war is no small job, but I do my best in this chapter.

In chapter 11, "The Open Forum as the Elder's Monastery," I discuss how your development as a facilitator is connected with your spiritual development.

The epilogue, "Keys to the Open Forum," summarizes methods and insights so that you can take them with you to your next small—or large—group meeting.

To mediate conflict, we need to remember that everything changes, the world is a dance, and we need to discover the steps trying to take place. Democratic rules of order, and the resulting organizational and legal procedures, are not enough. We need moment-to-moment awareness as well.

Things to Remember

1. Democracy without awareness can be tyranny. Without awareness, democracy adds to, but does not resolve, world problems.

2. Typical democratic procedures, such as *Robert's Rules of Order*, favor efficiency and repress feelings.

3. Deep democracy is a new awareness procedure that respects the diversity of individuals and perceives changing states of consciousness.

CHAPTER 2

The Open Forum
as Outer and Innerwork

The Open Forum is an ideal setting for a community to get to know
the rich diversity of ideas and feelings within its members. Forums are
public meeting places that host open discussions about community
problems. Open Forums can take place in town halls, on TV and radio
in your living room, in e-mail groups, or in the newspapers. Any group
can transform an Open Forum into an amazing ritual. Then your
school, business, or city colleagues can feel proud of themselves for
learning how to create community.

Take a tip from Aboriginal peoples who prepare feasts to mark the
beginning and completion of rituals where people speak with one
another, as in the Open Forum. Sharing food, having a party, and celebrating the group's diversity and accomplishments can enrich Open
Forums everywhere, especially in cities where people do not know one
another.

The Open Forum can become a magical space that welcomes
everyone's viewpoint on a particular problem. The participants of city
forums are usually folks who are touched by the issues at hand. These
folks may be "authorities" or "experts" in given areas who come with

prepared speeches. There are usually more than enough social activists fighting for their particular viewpoint, as well as quiet people who sit silently in the background, and political leaders hoping to be heard.

Different Types of Open Forum Processes

The Open Forum concept can be applied anywhere there are groups of people trying to work together. I have seen applications in schools, military groups, churches, multinational organizations, neighborhood disputes, and war zones. I use the term *Open Forum* to mean a relatively informal, open space and time for part of (or the whole of) organizations to meet for the purpose of solving problems and creating community.

The community ritual I am calling the Open Forum is an ancient ritual that has occurred in one form or another in most countries. Depending on the culture and the situation, most town meetings today aspire to be linear, one-dimensional formats for discussion. However, although linear discussions are important, they do not solve complex public or organizational problems, since such dilemmas and long-term difficulties always involve colorful, emotional, even traumatic experiences.

The history of Open Forums in the United States can be traced to eighteenth-century town meetings that were convened, in part, because the settlers felt distanced from England (*Washington Post* 1999). The need to lessen the sense of alienation from the "homeland" government spurred the creation of meetings wherein participants experienced the give-and-take of the governing process and empowered themselves by simply talking and listening. Open Forums, perhaps like all grassroots movements, are organized when there is too much distance from "the top" and too little distribution of power.

The methods of First Nation peoples have often been used as models for such meetings. For example, early colonists in the United States witnessed and tried to replicate the democracy, respect, and decorum found among Native American tribal council gatherings such as those held by the Iroquois. Later, Protestant sects, such as the Quakers, extended such procedures, creating their own methods of conducting meetings.

Nelson Mandela, in his *Long Walk to Freedom*, speaks of the Open Forum-styled meetings held by his tribe in South Africa. In his group, no decision was made until *everyone* had spoken.

Arnold Mindell, Ph.D.

*Some speakers rambled and never seemed to get to the point, others came to
the matter at hand directly and made a set of arguments succinctly and directly
. . . some speakers were emotional, others less so. . . . Democracy meant that all
men were to be heard and a decision was to be taken together as a people.
Majority rule was a foreign notion. . . . A minority was not to be crushed by a
majority. No conclusion was forced on people who disagreed. If no agreement
could be reached, another meeting would be called.*

Native Americans were also against voting and wanted instead to
talk. I should mention that town meetings such as those held in
ancient Greece, in Athens, discouraged the practice of voting. We
need to ask about the meaning of democracy in any tradition in which
"all men were to be heard."

The Moods behind the Open Forum

In addition to distance from the top and the need for a redistribu-
tion of power, the origins and need for Open Forums can be found in
the mood of a group.

Gossip: The very beginning stages of Open Forums occur when people gossip and begin to gather to discuss unsolved problems.
Alternatively, forums may arise spontaneously as informal gatherings
where folks discuss public events; only later do these become formal-
ized public meetings in the town, city, or on the Internet. Gossip is
important; it tells us that there is a kind of dreaming going on; things
are happening in the group, under the surface.

Frustration: Another impetus for town meetings comes from the
frustration felt by those without social power who feel afraid of those
at the top. Everyone has experienced this frustration in groups and
businesses, families and cities, at one time or another. This frustration
gets expressed in many ways, one of which is simply not participating
in government events such as voting. Many people who do not show
up for public events or vote in democratic countries boycott these
activities because they feel ignored by their leaders.

Hopelessness: At each trouble spot on the planet that I have worked
in, people felt hopeless about making change, though few openly

21

admitted that they felt this way. However, apathy prevails; you can feel it palpably in the low energy or sudden bursts of anger at town meetings, or by merely walking down the street in a given neighborhood. Hopelessness is epidemic in areas where people tend to be depressed in their schools and at their jobs. Hopelessness manifests in many ways, such as sickness, absenteeism, substance abuse, or anticipation of retirement or even death.

Open Forums directly address hopelessness by providing a venue for individuals to "speak their piece." In this way, individuals often feel heard, not only by those present at the meetings, but by others in their city or organization. In fact, in large town meetings, the news media functions as a connection to the rest of the organization or city. Individuals experience themselves as having an effect on the world. Open Forums can transform hopelessness into its opposite—excitement about being heard and making a difference. Forums are a powerful way for individuals to exert their influence on social change, which is always unfolding. Grassroots groups have initiated some of the greatest changes in societies! Remember the way in which the peace movements of the 1960s in the United States helped stop war in Vietnam. Remember history. Remember nonviolent conflict work. Remember the student sit-in movement and boycott that broke the system of segregation in Nashville, Tennessee; Gandhi's campaign against British rule in India; the consumer boycott campaigns against apartheid in South Africa; the valiant resistance of Danish citizens to Nazi invaders; Solidarity's factory occupations and strikes that won the right to free trade unions in Poland; and the people's movement that challenged and eventually defeated the dictatorship of General Augusto Pinochet in Chile.

The desire for community: The origin of many forums lies in the vision of participants who can see the potential for their organization to become more like a community involving not only all the people, but all parts of the environment as well.

Subtle Expectations of the Open Forum

By the time an Open Forum is about to begin, you as a facilitator need to know the overt as well as unexpressed expectations of the participants. Perhaps the main expectation is that we are going to do something, as in, "We, the people." It is not the government or boss who does things, but we, the people. The Open Forum is, in a way, an attempt to solve the hopelessness problem by restoring or inaugurating a ritual sense of community identity and empowerment. Here are two major expectations of an Open Forum.

First, more community, less fear and violence: Because traumatic and painful events are often the incentive for organizing Open Forums, an often unconscious or buried expectation is that there will be less gossip, less violence, and more community feeling as the immediate result. Open Forums can show us how to stop abusing the environment, and one another, by modeling awareness of moment-to-moment interactions on a person-to-person level.

However, leaders are usually not trained to utilize this type of awareness. For example, during an argument between two parties, audience members inevitably laugh at, or grumble about, one speaker and clap for another. The wise facilitator can make everyone aware of these moments by pointing out the humiliation that may be experienced by one side or another. In this way, forums reduce violence by pointing out the seeds of violence in subtle interactions. Only when humiliation is either "not noticed" or ignored, or when anger is not heard, does violence erupt. Groups both large (cities, towns, and organizations) and small (families) that process contentious moments minimize violence.

Second, education about communication: Wide-awake facilitators can point out to the public how communication can inadvertently hurt or help. The Open Forum teaches and models openness to diverse populations as a foundation for community consciousness.

The governing bodies of organizations that make policies around "hot" issues such as economy, sexism, homophobia, and racism, have no way of demonstrating what those policies *mean* to people in the midst of one-on-one interactions. For example, say there is a rule that everyone deserves respect, and there is a rule against ageism. However, if the adults ignore the impassioned speech of a young teenager, rules around "respect" have little meaning. The facilitator must point out that ageism—favoring one age group of people over another age group—is a moment-to-moment process as well as a social problem. In other words, the awareness work that you can demonstrate in Open Forums helps everyone actualize democratic concepts that governments are powerless to enforce.

Different Kinds of Public Meetings

There are many different styles and interesting methods that deal with groups. Most people have heard about group therapy with a dozen or so individuals interacting, hoping for personal change and/or the development of the group. Performance groups such as Dr. John L. Johnson's Washington, D.C., Playback Theater reenact personal and social scenes so that audiences can reexperience and better comprehend situations in their own lives, groups, and organizations. Conflict management groups come together to negotiate resolutions to tensions between various parties. Here the goal is usually the peaceful settlement of an issue, allowing both parties to feel that some of their needs have been met.

Process-oriented group work is worldwork, and the Open Forum is part of worldwork's spectrum. *Worldwork* is the broad term for community-making and conflict-resolving approaches to small and large groups (up to about one thousand people) based on deep democracy. Worldwork has been created to deal with communities that are in balance as well as in wildly chaotic states of transformation. On the one side of the worldwork spectrum are negotiation procedures and business meetings, where immediate solutions to problems are the focus. On the other side of the spectrum are large group interactions occurring "in the round," where emotional, sometimes traumatic, deep-seated issues are processed. The goal here is exposition and discovery, not immediate resolution.

Process-oriented Open Forums lie between business meetings and large, open, emotional meetings. The Open Forum is more dramatic than standard business meetings, yet more linear than the ongoing worldwork group processes. People with more mainstream education, often approach emotional issues with a sort of "classist" attitude: "Why is everyone always so emotional and irrational!" Worldwork understands classist (or elitist) attitudes, but also accepts the basic emotional substratum of human nature that makes all of us upset, angry, and emotional at times. To invalidate this substratum can be racist and marginalizes the passion that fuels what we all want and don't want. Open Forums are usually brief, lasting about two hours. In contrast, the large-group format of worldwork encourages whole communities to gather together from three to six hours a day, for several days, to reduce tension and to create greater awareness of communication styles. Of course, conducting worldwork in the large-group format depends on the situation; the essence of emotional issues may be addressed head-on, or, depending on the culture, may be gently approached by encouraging people to create fairy-tale solutions to the problems at hand.

An Example from Dublin

Sometimes the Open Forum is connected to large-group, community-styled worldwork meetings. Several years ago, my partner, Amy, and I were invited by people connected with the city government of Belfast to hold an Open Forum and worldwork training in an attempt to reduce the number of bombings that occur yearly, each time different groups celebrate their history.* Because the lives of the organizers in Belfast who were setting up the meeting were endangered, at the last minute, the worldwork setting was moved to Dublin and organized by the process-workers of that city.

Imagine the setting. Several hundred people gathered in downtown Dublin. Politicians and ordinary citizens from Northern Ireland and from the Republic of Ireland came together in the Samuel Beckett Theatre, around the time of the voting to accept or reject the "peace accord." The tension was palpable as the conference began. We first asked invited speakers from the various sides in Northern Ireland and the Republic of Ireland to give five-minute speeches describing their diverse views about the situation.

Immediately after these talks, the proceedings were opened up to the

---

*I discuss other aspects of this example in *Dreaming While Awake*, p. 194-195.

public. We used the Open Forum format, in which people sat in concentric circles. At first, we asked individuals to voice their viewpoints, first those in the north who wanted to break with the Republic of Ireland, then those from the south who wanted Ireland to rid itself of the British.

Suddenly two men, vehemently representing the opposition between the south and the north, arose and began yelling at one another from opposite sides of the circle. (To protect the individuals involved, I speak of the conflict simply in terms of the south and the north. My reason for doing this is that I am not primarily interested in examining the specific details of the conflict, its historical or geographic characteristics, but in the generally human nature of conflict *processes*. In this example, I am focusing on the Irish group; however, similar conflicts with the same structures happen everywhere and are independent of nationality.) Soon, everyone was out of their seats as these two came into the center of the large circle. They stood face to face, locked in the most antagonistic dialogue. The situation became dramatic, painful, and even terrifying as the whole group stood with them, taking sides, calling out their support for one man and then the other.

At one moment, as those two courageous people were yelling at one another, I recall that either Amy or I yelled at the top of our voices, using microphones to be heard, "Please be careful!" The man from the south reacted. He turned around to face us and asked, "Are you crazy? I have not spoken to a man from the north for twenty-five years! I am not going to calm down now!"

We understood and retreated. The emotions on both sides escalated as the opponents in the center told about killings and traumatic events in which their opponents had bombed or shot their group or family members. Everyone in the room started to speak at once.

At some point, I remembered to use my awareness and watch for body signals. Above the din, I noticed that the neck of one of the spokesmen had become exceedingly red. I yelled out, "Your neck is red." To my great surprise, he quieted down for a moment, turned toward me and, in a room that had fallen suddenly silent, said, "Of course it is red! I have lethally high blood pressure, and my doctor warned me to stay away from here." Almost before he could complete his sentence, the man from the other side said, "Who are you to talk? You are not the only one who is suffering. I had three heart attacks this last month, and my doctor told me not to come here today!"

Everyone in that large auditorium remained silent as the two opponents just stared at one another. I can hardly describe my surprise and amazement when the man from the south, with the red blotch on his neck, went over to the man from the north and, slowly and gently, put an arm around his shoulders. There they stood, two men, side by side in the center of the circle, with their heads bowed toward the floor.

These two men modeled a coming together that was unthinkable under the circumstances. The entire auditorium of people remained quiet, then resumed working, peacefully together now, to find a way to live together. All the while, those two men sat near one another on the outside of the circle. The next evening, the people of Ireland voted in favor of the peace accord.

I really do not understand why this event came out so well; it was surely due to the moment in history, and the courage and wisdom of those two men and the people in that auditorium. Was that group process a foreshadowing of events to come? In any case, awareness of signals seemed to play a crucial role in the outcome.

If Amy or I had been able to be really awake, with full access to our awareness, we would have heard them mention the ghosts of the dead in their first angry descriptions of the situation. After all, they had already told terrible stories of their friends and relatives who had been killed in violent acts of revenge from the other side. Having heard about the dead could have led me to bring in the topic of death earlier. Nevertheless, though I missed the mentioning of the dead as they yelled at each other, I did not miss death as it appeared in the body signal of the man's neck. Awareness brought out the "dreaming," the common ground, the body problems that indicated the nearness of death.

A favorite image of the Haida people, living on the Queen Charlotte Islands comes to mind: In some ways, we humans are like separate trees, standing proudly above the ground while our roots entangle indistinguishably beneath the ground.

I will speak more about awareness skills and methods in the next chapters. Here I simply want to remind the reader that process-oriented worldwork is really a continuum with at least three formats: business-styled negotiation and community-making procedures, Open Forum work, and large-group emotional work. These formats overlap and can be combined, as occurred in the Dublin group, where a large-group interaction followed an Open Forum setting.

The Worldwork Spectrum

Little or No Awareness of Feelings:
Business meetings, linear processes that use known rules and procedures.

Awareness of Emotions:
The Open Forum semilinear processes, the central focus of the present book. These can be used anytime.

Powerful Emotional Transformation:
Large group, nonlinear process for use during community-making times or extreme crisis periods.

Open Forum and/or Large-Group Work:

Some combination of the Open Forum and large-group work usually works well in very tense, riot-like situations or war zones. As I have said before, while large-group formats are often dramatic and emotional, usually lasting between three hours and seven days, the Open Forum tends to be more focused and more linear. It is best suited for business organizations and open townlike meetings.

In this book, I focus mainly on the Open Forum because of its wide application and *preventative* value: If it is used regularly, many (perhaps all) of the more extreme situations may be avoided. The semilinear process of Open Forums is progressive: There is a beginning, a conflict, and, often, an end or resolution. For example, a problem is stated and methods of dealing with that problem are explored. Then, dialogue that allows unpredictable emotional interchange can emerge. Finally, this interchange is followed by proposals gained from insights into existing diversity factors and prior experiences with the current tension. Nonlinear group processes enable participants to focus more deeply on the emotional substratum of the issues, allowing the feelings that are present to unfold. Nonlinear worldwork processes require more training, centering, and knowledge of extreme states as well as the psychological dynamics of organizations.

Getting around Your Fear

Regardless of the exact format, one of a facilitator's biggest problems is her own fear of the situation. Because of existing tensions, facilitating process-oriented Open Forums can be very challenging. A community uses conflict to discover its parts and to get to know itself better. Thus, creating a safe space where people feel free to speak requires being able to create a "container" for people so that they can go through complex, emotional territory. But before everyone feels safe, and respected, submerged topics inevitably arise.

Although you may want to conduct an Open Forum, those submerged topics can make you feel uneasy. The beginning facilitator is often afraid of the conflict, fears being attacked, and cringes at the thought of being publicly shamed. Even more advanced facilitators want to run for the hills when a conflict comes up! Conflicts can be scary.

A few tips may help if you would like to conduct an Open Forum but feel shy about doing so. The first tip is that noticing fear is part of the overall awareness work. If you are afraid, then consider the possibility that your fear can be part of the solution. If you are aware of your fear and bring it into the group as a role that others can feel as well, then not only fear but the powers that terrify people can be *revealed*. In this way, your fear can lead to greater caring and more respect for the powers that be.

In fact, your fear (or courage) may be just what your organization is neglecting to recognize. The organization needs *you* to lead Open Forums, without changing your basic nature. You don't have to act more courageous than you are. Your own personality will be one of the keys to the conflict work.

The more you try to push a group, the more it seems like a sailboat being run by people with oars in hand. If you use awareness, the sail catches the wind and nature moves everything along. Relax, the wind will take us all where we need to be going. Follow yourself, but try not to forget to follow nature as well. In summary then:

If you are afraid of	**Then consider that**
Conflict	You may be feeling the role of fear that others have as well
Not having enough courage, or not being able to save the situation	You need awareness, not power, to notice and follow the changes that are inherent in all life forms

What Are Your Personal Goals in Facilitating an Open Forum?

Before beginning an Open Forum, you need to be clear about your own personal goals. One of my colleagues, John Johnson, suggested forming a "clearness committee" (a Quaker term) to help get clear about what we are doing when we embark on this activity. What is it you are looking for?

Do you want peace and harmony?

Do you want to be better known?

Do you want to change or save someone?

Are you a social activist and want to change a part of the community?

Do you want to help people?

Identify your goals clearly, then explore the degree to which your goals intersect with those in the community as a whole. Who shares and does not share your goals? How do your goals coincide with or differ from the goals of the people who are coming to the forum? If you are not clear about the possible one-sided nature of your goals, you will be shocked later to discover that some people (from another side) in the community have rejected you. Without knowing it, you rejected them first.

For example, one facilitator told me her goal was to become better known as an arbitrator by negotiating a dispute between two large businesses. The members of those groups felt her pushing them instead of following their signals and fired her on the spot! This facilitator felt rejected without realizing that her goals inadvertently rejected the needs of the business people.

Being rejected is neither good nor bad; it is merely a sign that you were not working for the whole community, only for parts of it. This one-sidedness is inevitable, since you (and your team) are one individual (and one little group). You cannot have the same feelings as everyone else. On the other hand, if you are not clear about your one-sidedness, it will re-create conflict. If you are conscious of the one-sided nature of your goals, you can use them during the forum as an asset.

For example, you might support that part of the community that shares your goals and support the dialogue with the members from the "other" side who have other opinions. If you are not clear about your goals, you might begin to think the community is not ready for your way of thinking, or that some people are just unconscious or "bad."

Know the group; know their beliefs, their problems, their styles. Do they all talk at once, or are they quiet? What's their style, their lingo? How many are present? And what is your time commitment? Is your work a one-time affair, or is it ongoing? Find out what methods they are now using for conducting meetings so you can build your method into theirs, so that you collaborate and do not insult their current procedures.

Who Has Hired or Supports You?

If you are part of the community you are going to work with, and have hired yourself, so to speak, then clarity about your goals is especially important. If others in an organization hired you, you need to know the goals they hope you will fulfill. Remember however, that to fulfill anyone's goals best, usually *everyone's* must be met. You are like a doctor who must attend to a body. If the liver is calling for help, you must help the liver. But ultimately, the life of the liver depends on the wellness of the heart, the kidneys, and all the other organs.

Innerwork Preparation

Now that you are clear about your goals for the forum and the goals for those who hired you, your next step in preparing for the Open Forum is to know how you yourself are an Open Forum. What parts of yourself are going to be called into action by this forum? How might you be in conflict with other parts of yourself? To feel centered and be able to use your awareness, some form of innerwork is needed. After all, your very interest in an Open Forum means that you are thinking of the people as being outside yourself and not inner figures within your own being.

Regardless of whether you like some and fear others, everyone is a part of you! (If you don't believe me, just wait for your dreams tonight or your friends tomorrow who accuse you of the same things you thought were true of the "others.") In other words, when you do an Open Forum, you are helping yourself as much as you are helping an organization. In at least one way, there is no one to help besides yourself! To understand the organization's diversity, understand your diversity. Outer change happens most rapidly when it is modeled by individuals who themselves are living democracies. The more you know and are open to your own inner conflicts, the more people will accept you as a helper.

The most helpful idea I know of for clearing out your mind and preparing for the Open Forum is to consider that the Open Forum you want to facilitate is entirely within yourself. Take a moment and try the following suggestions for innerwork. If one of my suggestions does not quite fit you, let your mind amend it accordingly. If you are working with teammates, one of you can ask the other the following questions.

1. Imagine the coming (or a possible) Open Forum. If you are not preparing for one in the moment, imagine one, think of an issue important to you that you would like to see processed in an Open Forum. What issue comes to mind just now?

2. Imagine two speakers who come forward to dialogue about the issue at stake. Give these two people names, Ms. You and Mr. Other. Now imagine the Open Forum and these two speakers. Let's say that each speaker talks for one minute. Listen quietly to what each has to say. Let each side speak deeply about her or his point of view. (Make notes.) Let each side speak about what is essential to him or her. What are the basic points each side is trying to make?

   Ms. You: _____

   Mr. Other: _____

3. Now ask yourself: "How do the two sides represent different aspects of my own thinking, behavior, and deep-seated feelings? Which side or view would I like to be more conscious of in the future? How can I be open to and understand this side of myself?" Does your imaginary Open Forum reflect inner problems you have recently been thinking about? Open Forums can be a powerful method of discovering what is happening deep within yourself.

4. Also ask yourself how the imaginary Open Forum reflects relationship issues you have been thinking about. What side have you been on inside yourself, and how does your one-sidedness help to create problems? What would you like to change, if anything, in your own life as a result of this innerwork, in this next few minutes and in the coming week?

The point of this exercise is to get clear in yourself about who you are and how you are the world. If you are open to yourself, you will feel better and be more open to others as well. With a more solid *inner* foundation, we can now begin to lay the groundwork and prepare for the outer event, the Open Forum.

Things to Remember

1. If you strive to do too much, you may be relying on power instead of awareness. Insecurity occurs if you try to do something

without *feeling* inspired. We do not need you as a leader for world change. Change is inherent in people and nature. You need awareness, not power, to notice and follow the changes.

2. If you are afraid, use your fear as a role in the process. Your role of fear can lead to greater caring and more respect. In fact, your fear (or courage) can be just what your organization is denying or marginalizing. The organization needs *you, with all your fears,* to lead Open Forums without changing your basic nature. You don't have to act more courageous than you are. Your own personality is a key to conflict work.

3. One of the goals of the Open Forum is to gain a vivid sense of "We, the people." It isn't the government. The Open Forum is, in a way, an attempt to solve the hopelessness problem.

4. Open Forums give individuals hope by creating the chance for direct impact on the media and the powers that govern us. We need to remember that grassroots groups initiate political changes in the world!

5. The Open Forum shows how to stop abuse taking place in a given moment on a person-to-person level, which is something a government is not able to do. It doesn't know how to do that. It can only make rules. It cannot make people become conscious of their actions and their consequences.

6. Be clear about your personal goals. Do you want global peace? Do you want to be better known as a facilitator? Are you in the social activist goal/position and want to change a part of the community? Be clear about your goals, then explore the degree to which your goals intersect with those in the community as a whole. Who does and does not share your goals? How do your goals coincide with or differ from those of the people who are coming to the forum? If you are not clear about the possible one-sided nature of your goals, your community may become your opponent.

7. To lay a solid foundation of inner awareness and clarity about the contents of your own psyche, conduct an imaginary Open Forum as if all the players and their opposing viewpoints represent aspects of yourself.

CHAPTER 3

The Open Forum
as Groupwork

Once you know your own goals, it is time to delve deeper into your preparation. How you work at the Open Forum depends completely on your culture, ethnic background, gender, age, style, health, and how you feel about the topics at hand. The comments I make about preparation cover only those issues encountered by everyone who confronts the challenges of making or facilitating public presentations.

To begin with, think about your global goals, your greatest dreams. What is the most wonderful result you hope to accomplish with your work—the outcome you are almost too shy to admit even to yourself. What are those goals? Write them down now. These great dreams give you the power and courage to do public work. Be as clear as you can about your hopes. Here are some of my goals.

One-in-a-Hundred Consciousness

Government people from Norway who were trying to create peace in Kosovo during the war asked me why international peacemaking committees were not succeeding. They wanted to know, "What kind of facilitators get the best and quickest results?" I had to think long and hard. I realized that the right facilitators have skills to deal with moment-to-moment interactions and the global, long-term goals that enable them to make the best use of these skills. The most important long-term goal that I know of is *awareness of one's own nature*. Then I think of the community's awareness of its nature, and its different parts, its ghosts and roles.

At least one facilitator in a large group must be aware of what is going on in herself and her community. I call this awareness *One-in-a-Hundred Consciousness*. The effect of such a person on a group is immeasurably important. If only one person in a hundred perceives the subtler undertone of what is transpiring and can articulate it in a meaningful way to all, the group feels safer, people feel respected, and the meeting works. But sometimes it is not easy to find such "elders" who are aware of the diversity and who can speak about the different sides in a kind, detached, and open manner.

Such elders have a goal I refer to as *you today and me tomorrow*. This means that there is at least one person in a hundred at any given moment who remembers, "Today you may look troubled or nuts. You are crazy, you want to kill, and you hate others. But *tomorrow*, I might be just like you." If I can tell that you know that I am upset today, but that tomorrow, it could be you who is angry and hurt, then whatever my issue and state of mind, I will surely respect and listen to you.

If you model, as a facilitator, *you today and me tomorrow*, all will feel that you have love and understanding for this troubled, violent state in which group members find themselves.

Developing this attitude is a challenge. You need to remember how easy it is to get upset with someone in a conflict. Remember how you thought they should be different, and *they* should deal with their conflict better. Recall conflicts in your own life, how upset you were, and you will know that the people you thought were not dealing with conflict well are really mirrors of parts of yourself you have tried to forget.

Things to Notice

Let's assume that you are this one person in one hundred who

36

comes forth in your community, church, high school, business, or town and says compassionately, "I notice . . . this and that." What have you noticed? In addition to whatever insights you get about the *content* of what is being said, you also notice the *process*, which is composed, in part, of roles played by people. **A person is more than a role.** You realize that a person is more complete, more diverse than the momentary role he or she is playing. You can see that there is an oppressor, for example, but that oppressor is a role, and the person playing it is more than that one role. There may be a victim in pain, but the person in pain has many other sides to herself as well.

You notice ghost roles—that is, events or people who are mentioned but who are not present—and you name and represent them as an actor might do, then play out or explain their role. Ghosts are to organizations as dream figures are to an individual dream: figments of our imaginations, patterns of our everyday behavior of which we are unconscious. Every mention of history or the future, of things not present, is a ghost. For example, in the Open Forum in Ireland, the dead were ghost roles. At some point, I could have taken on the role of the dead or dying, and said, "I have been injured and am dying, this is killing me . . . etc."

Later, I will talk about the details involved in the facilitator's awareness work. I just want to begin to whet your appetite for awareness at this early point.

Awareness, not only power, is needed. As a wide-awake facilitator, you may or may not have the power to speak out. Power is less important than awareness. If you have awareness, you do not need power. You need power and courage only if you are fighting something. Awareness does not fight; it may notice fighting and other things happening, but it does not identify with or judge those things. When awareness is present, the spontaneous behavior of everyone is awakened and unpredictable processes emerge that are what's best for all. In the example of the Open Forum in Ireland, I spoke about the body gestures of the man with lethal blood pressure, and how noticing those gestures led to the common ground between opposing parties.

When awareness is present, process is its own solution. Chaos is only a momentary process in which awareness has not yet been used. When awareness is used, as in the Irish conflict, the process is its own solution.

If you hope that the whole community or the whole of humanity is going to become conscious, you will never get anything done. The project is too big. Furthermore, if everyone were enlightened, it would be boring. It is more fun if you are conscious one minute in a hundred. Someone else can do the job in the next minute.

Facilitators appreciate diversity. Bringing consciousness of diversity to the foreground eventually helps everyone. Early in an Open Forum, such a facilitator might say, "I notice we have a diverse community; there are people of this opinion and some of that opinion. Notice the various ages, races, and economic situations of all those who are present. There are some whose diversity has not yet been demonstrated." Every forum is filled with amazing people, roles, and dreams!

Community Goals

After getting clear about your personal goals, you need to ask community members about *their* goals. How do you find out the goals of a community in tension? You—and/or members of your team—need to speak with people from the various sides of the issue ahead of time. This takes time, and in some cases, legwork. You have to visit some people and have a face-to-face discussion. Ask about their goals. Are they interested in feeling safer? Do they want a greater sense of community? What are the diversity issues, economic issues, class problems? Here are some steps:

Get the facts. Find out about the cultural histories of the people involved. If possible, research the past stories told about the business, school, or spiritual community. How and when was it founded? What is its reason for being? These stories are like myths; they contain patterns that may still be working today. If you know the myth or story of a community, members will feel better understood. Once you have the story, tell it to some group or community member to test its accuracy. For example, I once put together the myth of one group after hearing many individual stories. The myth went something like this: "Like the king's council, we are a mighty organization influencing countless millions. We can solve all human problems but one. One of the king's sons has fallen ill and is killing us, one by one, with his magical sword. Sad to say, there is none among us who can stop him. Let's call some grand wizards. Hopefully they will survive the meeting with him, and bring the council and land back to order again."

The story is crucial, because it is part of the group's dreaming, the impulse that brought it to birth and sustains it today. The story contains suggestions about what is missing today, and why the problems of today exist. It is also important to study the historical context from different viewpoints: legal, economic, civil rights, etc. If you are working on an environmental issue, find out about the natural resources of the area and even the religious or mythical background. Know and respect people's beliefs about the Earth and appreciate the economic reasons that, for some, justify using the environment. Learn about the native people and their stories from that region of the world.

Learn the demographics. You also need to find out about the demographics, the statistical characteristics of the human population involved in the issue that is the focus of the Open Forum: the numbers of people involved, their ages, incomes, gender, race, and so forth. How many people are involved with one side of the issue, and how many people are involved with the other side?

Study the umbrella. The issue your community may be working on could be finances, employment, racism, homophobia, sexism, power imbalance, gossip, safety, or others. Any given organizational issue is a label—a crucial label—people have assigned to identify what is troubling the group just now. At the same time, the label is an umbrella covering many subsidiary issues that are intimately connected to the issue being discussed. You also need to know something about the subsidiary issues; otherwise, they will arise and detract attention from the main issue. To avoid this derailment, you can choose to focus on the main issue, then look into a subsidiary issue at another point or in another forum.

For example, say there is a conflict between two leading people in your organization. It turns out that the president is a man and the vice president is a woman. In this example, the label for the issue is "conflict at the top," but one of the subsidiary issues under that umbrella (conflict at the top) is likely to be sexism. If the people are of different races, racism may also be involved. Political correctness can also be a subsidiary issue. Does awareness of difference inhibit or enable deeper interactions?

Most conflict resolution procedures and peacemaking methods focus on the umbrella issue without researching it sufficiently and realizing that the issue is an umbrella, not a solid piece of rock. In any one community, or while working on any one issue, you need to remember that each person has his or her own issue under any one umbrella. There is a diversity of issues under any one umbrella, and your research needs to reveal these issues and incorporate their significance.

One of the deepest principles of the Open Forum, and of all group processes, is that no single issue can ever be completely resolved unless all the subsidiary issues are addressed at one time or another. In a later chapter I will discuss how to remember and frame all the issues and, at the same time, how to focus on one at a time.

In the beginning of an Open Forum, you might use your research and tell people about the umbrella. For example, say your research has revealed to you that the umbrella issue is "conflict at the top," yet you are aware that there are other issues in the background that may or may not get air time (such as sexism and/or racism, perhaps homophobia, or classism, or economics). Once you bring these subsidiary issues out into the open, people do not have to break into explosive arguments to make sure that their issues are heard.

Knowing about how subsidiary issues interact is very important. For example, I remember a large number of people gathering at the Process Work Center in Portland, Oregon, to discuss conflicts between the homeless and the business people in our neighborhood. City authorities, the police, business people, and a number of homeless folks all came to represent their viewpoints. Some were sober, and some were drunk.

Looking back, I realize that I was not sufficiently aware of the umbrella situation. I knew a lot about the homeless, and the viewpoints of the business people and police, but I was not prepared for the interaction between homelessness and the psychiatric community. It turned out that the lack of facilities and distribution of medication were big issues. A lot of the homeless are homeless in part because of lack of distribution of psychiatric medication. I did not realize that, according to *The Oregonian* (Oregon's most popular newspaper), there is a lack of social funding for psychiatric care facilities. As a result, for every ten ill people accepted at one caretaking facility in Portland, forty people are turned away.

I was prepared for the subsidiary interaction between homelessness and economics, and between homelessness and race, but I was not thinking enough about the connection between homelessness, drug problems, and social psychiatry. As a result, when the homeless complained about the lack of psychiatric medication available to them, I could only follow and facilitate the resulting interactions in the forum, and not truly participate in them myself. I prefer to feel everything deeply, and not only help from the outside.

So if you are facilitating an Open Forum on sexism, for example, remember the diverse issues under that one umbrella. Because of racism, women of color and white women are not always in agreement about what the problems are around sexism because the issues and concerns of people of color and white people are radically different. Similarly, research will inform you that focusing on sexism only in connection with relationships between women and men marginalizes gay relationships. The more general issue is the conflicting social ideas about what constitute female and male attributes. Furthermore, sexism as an *internalized reality* is another layer of the issue that is often overlooked.

At one Open Forum in the United States conducted by members of our organization on the topic of sexism, under the umbrella of sexism we noticed issues of racism, and under that was the issue of beauty. In a relatively large group, gathered together in the midst of the city, Asian, Asian American, Mexican, African American, and Hispanic spoke about how mainstream white standards marginalize everyone else. In addition, subsidiary issues abounded. There were many feelings expressed about women being ignored in business, prejudice against women from lower economic groups, stories of domestic violence and abuse, and pain from collective standards for appearance.

Near the end of that Open Forum, the atmosphere relaxed as people began to speak personally about their lives. Among several women who spoke, a young teenager talked about having an "only-women's-party" celebrating her first menstrual period. Her sense of pride in being a woman touched the hearts of everyone! Because we held closely to the topic of sexism, yet were aware that subsidiary topics might arise, the large group that gathered at the Open Forum felt like a community, despite the intensely diverse viewpoints around race and economics.

If you are not clear about the subsidiary issues under the umbrella topic, you may find yourself sideswiped. You begin the Open Forum by focusing on the stated issue, then someone representing a group or issue that you forgot comes forward and attacks you for marginalizing them. Then, in spite of your good intentions, there you are, being attacked and looking embarrassed. Instead of being the helpful facilitator you wanted to be, you have suddenly become a victim of the very people you were hoping to empower!

The moral of the story is "Know what's under the umbrella" ahead of time, and when a subsidiary issue arises, frame it. For example, in the forum on sexism, one woman complained that she was not compensated equally with men for her job. At this very moment, another participant raised her hand to speak and seemed to change the subject, discussing how much worse things were for older women regarded as "over the hill." You might then say, "Oh, here is the topic of ageism," and so forth.

The title of the forum. Now that you have researched the main topic and all subsidiary issues, it is time to name the Open Forum, for you must advertise the forum to gather people. The title is important to think about. For example, if you do a forum on *sexism*, you may be perceived as already taking sides. Some men will assume that you are saying *they* are sexist. They will not assume that you are interested in their viewpoints, but that you are a social activist looking for someone's head to chop off. If you want to hold an organizational or town or city meeting on sexism with all the groups present who are needed to change the situation, call the forum, "Women! We shall focus on the issues of women and men in school or the workplace," or something like that.

Identify and speak with the trusted elders. Elders are not just the bosses; they are folks, young or old, who are respected by the various, diverse subgroups of the larger community. In given settings, it may even be important to invite the elders to sit with the facilitators at the front, showing the community that you do support its diversity. Martha Sandbower, one of our staff, wrote: "One thing I learned from you that was helpful with kids in a school system was to have the teachers sit next to me as the facilitator. It helped me to get respect. With kids who don't know you, this respect is crucial."

Before beginning the forum, it is important to talk with the elders about who and what has been marginalized in their groups. In dealing with schools, find out which kids are respected most by others, and ask them about school problems. In businesses, ask respected workers from each level to help with the forum. In city forums, ask respected elders from various economic classes, racial, gender, and sexual orientation groups to help. That is how you can be best prepared.

Choose a good location. Location makes a difference. Choose a location for the forum that is within easy reach of those for whom transportation is problematic. Choose a location that symbolizes the diversity of the situation, such as a room or building on the edge between two parts of a city, or a place that has already been used in the past for community-making projects.

Timing: Good for whom? We once chose the University of Houston as the setting for a forum on the issue of racial killing in the Southern part of the United States. The choice of the location made a lot of sense from many viewpoints, but we had forgotten to consider the fact that the forum was being held on the first day of classes at the beginning of a new semester in Houston! Many people came, but the students made us realize that we had forgotten that even more would have come if it had not been the first day of school.

Advertising is important. A warm, personal, friendly invitation is important. If you are a social activist, you might want to advertise your work in a manner that blasts the mainstream. But then you are in con-flict before you begin, and the mainstream may not appear! You had best work on how *you yourself are mainstream*, before creating that activist ad; otherwise, only other activists will come. That can be an important outcome—but be sure it is the one you want.

Where to advertise. Place ads within the organization you are working for. Or, if the Open Forum takes place in a city, place ads in all the newspapers—in all the newspapers, not only mainstream daily, but in journals related to each side of the issue. If you have the funds, place announcements with radio stations and attempt to get some form of TV coverage. Many stations will advertise the forum for nothing if it is clearly for the benefit of the public. Use the Internet and e-mail. In your advertisement, include, at least, something like the following information.

Title:	Women and Men
Theme:	Women's issues!
Timing:	7:00 p.m. to 9:30 p.m.
Style:	Though we will stick to the topic, we are open to related themes and feelings. The forum will be more interactive than the town meetings you may have seen on TV.
Invited speakers:	The following speakers have been invited to "jump-start" the process by talking for a few minutes at the beginning of the forum.
Safety:	The facilitators will do their utmost to respect and protect everyone, regardless of their viewpoints on the topic.

Then comes the all-important "legwork." In speaking with the individuals you would like to invite, show them that you are interested in their viewpoints; let them know that divergent viewpoints may arise, but that you will try to facilitate the meeting in such a way that everyone will feel respected. A great deal of the work of the Open Forum is done in this preparatory stage when you convey, "Your viewpoint is needed," and "I want to make it safe for you to speak."

People generally feel unsafe bringing viewpoints out into the open, especially on controversial issues. You need to work with people on the phone to increase their comfort level—and it takes time to do this. You need to be aware that your own opinions are just one part of the issue. Otherwise, you may find it difficult to speak with folks who hold opinions that are very different from your own. I remember talking with the OCA, the Oregon Citizen's Alliance, a right-wing group against gay rights. I remember a colleague, Dawn Menken, telling me that in calling these folks, she could not even use the term "diversity"; it had no meaning for them. She had to tell them that their viewpoint was really important, that they were too often portrayed in the media as being the "enemy," and that the Open Forum might help their profile.

At the forum, subsidiary issues arose. The OCA spokesperson said, "We are afraid of the media; we are afraid the other side will publicly put us down." The elders in the lesbian/gay community said the same thing essentially. "We are afraid the other side will publicly hurt us." Here was the common ground—feelings of apprehension. It made us realize that, although the umbrella was sexual orientation, subsidiary issues involved the media and fear of attack.

While you are encouraging people to come, acknowledge the possible diversity of interests and viewpoints that they might encounter. Sense the fears and hopes of the people you wish to invite and let them know that you are aware of their fears. Tell them their viewpoints are part of community process and therefore crucial to the Open Forum and that you hope they will represent their ideas.

The people you speak to can help you do the necessary outreach before the forum. Ask them who to contact, whom they would like to see there, what magazines and papers they read; ask about websites, and the like. Follow your intuition; call the top rank as well as those lower down in your city, business, or school hierarchy.

Discover existing Open Forums. All groups, organizations, and communities have methods to deal with your particular topic. Whether you are part of the community or not, find out how the community has dealt with the issues until now. Were there open or secret meetings? Ask if the community has special festivals, or rituals. Try to support past or current open community dialogue programs, community mediation, or town hall meetings. You might want to mention and thank these programs when your Open Forum begins.

Now you can learn about the methods used by these programs, because your present work can build on already existing rituals and institutions. For instance, Portland has a nationally famous grassroots neighborhood association organization, and the first community mediation program in the country. Networking with existing programs always leads to useful collaboration, today and in the future.

How Does the Public See You?

Now that you have done some innerwork and have invited speakers, a next step is to get clear about how you are seen by the public. You need to find out from your friends, acquaintances, and co-workers how you appear in public. What do you look like to other people? Finding this out could be a big shock to you!

How are you seen in terms of your . . .

- ◆ Gender
- ◆ Race
- ◆ Age
- ◆ Health
- ◆ Social rank
- ◆ Education
- ◆ Profession
- ◆ Sexual orientation
- ◆ Religion
- ◆ Language

You should first answer these questions yourself, then ask others as well. You need to know *how* you are perceived and discuss those perceptions with others so that you are less surprised by participants' reactions. When you begin an Open Forum, talk about your appearance; it makes people feel more at home. Are you a person of color working in a community of white folks? A white person working in a community of people of color? A man talking about women's issues? A woman talking about men's issues? A teacher speaking about students' issues? Identify your context, study it, and talk about your position. Be clear about how others see your social rank and standing in a given community; acknowledge that how you are seen influences how you behave and how others might treat you.

For example, as a white, educated, middle-aged, heterosexual male, I have a great deal of social status in many places. Yet, when dealing with high school problems, sexism, racism, or homophobia, I can easily be seen as the "oppressor." Knowing and feeling this complex identification might lower my sense of self-esteem. This is not necessarily a negative development, especially if my self-esteem was unconsciously based mainly on being an educated, white, middle-class, heterosexual male. In fact, knowing how I appear allows me to say, for example, "I myself am a member of a potentially hurtful group. This makes me feel badly about myself and could reduce my abilities as a facilitator. Hopefully, you will support me in learning to use my awareness, as well as my social powers, for the benefit of all."

You should be clear, as well, about your own suffering in relation to the situation at hand or to other experiences. For example, I suffer and have suffered from anti-Semitism because of my Jewish background. This suffering can also be a source of support for my work in an Open Forum on social issues. I might say, for example (in an area that is not overtly anti-Semitic), "Hopefully my experiences and suffering as a Jewish person will enable me to be open to the problems of all."

The point is relativity. Notice that you are a man working on women's issues, a woman working in an essentially male organization, a foreigner in the country you are trying to be helpful in, a younger person working with older folks, or an older person with younger folks.

Whom to Invite?

Starting Open Forums with invited speakers can be helpful to jump-start the process. Then open the floor to everyone else.

Invite speakers from several sides of the issue. The speakers will bring forth some of the diverse positions that may be present in the audience. Choose speakers from the most extreme positions you can find on the issue because, otherwise, the extreme positions become ghosts that hover over and threaten the situation from the background. For example, in a forum on race in the United States, you might possibly invite a speaker from the Ku Klux Klan (a white, frequently violent, Aryan group that is against racial integration). Don't forget the Black Panthers,[1] as well as others from more median positions. If speakers are well known, they will attract the rest of the organization and city. The more extreme the positions, the more radical aspects you can bring in—which also increases interest.

Identify Team Goals

In preparing the groundwork, you need to think not only about yourself, but also about your facilitation team. How much help is needed? Do you have enough folks onboard to help? Does the team reflect the diversity of viewpoints that exists, the organization, and Open Forum issues? Who is best at the legwork? Who has the best contacts in the school, business, or city? After getting clear about yourself (see the exercise at the end of chapter 2), ask your co-workers to get clear about themselves as well.

Sometimes in training seminars for worldwork, our team consists of a diverse group of fifty individuals working with three hundred people. I have worked alone, as a member of a couple with Amy, and with teams of three to fifty. One thing I have learned is that the problems of the group always touch the team members.

As a supervisor, I can say that every team is touched by the conflicts it meets in the world. That is because each of us, as individuals and as a team, has the exact same conflicts that we are trying to resolve in the world. So, just as you must do your innerwork as an individual to discover the Open Forum as a process within yourself (as you did in chapter 2), the team as a unit needs to explore its collective experience of the forum issues.

Each member of an Open Forum team does some form of internal work to see how the outside is inside him or her. For a team to work effectively, each must work on a one-to-one basis with other members on relationship issues. Furthermore, members need to make time to process their own issues as a group. Each member must express all of his or her feelings on a given topic. Otherwise, existing relationship issues or unresolved feelings about the forum's topic can disorient the team during the Open Forum. In any case, unresolved conflicts within the team are not a sign that the group is "bad"—in fact, just the opposite. Unresolved issues can be used by the team members to model how such conflicts can be worked on when the open public forum occurs.

The team members need to hold each other accountable for the social analysis homework. In a diverse team, members can help one another with this homework. At best, team members model the world they want to create. Ideally, Open Forum teams look something like a basketball team—where members throw the ball back and forth, and not one, but all, are responsible for making a "basket"—a satisfactory world for all. Even after the Open Forum, the "basketball team" needs to go on learning, debriefing, and processing what has occurred.

Once you know yourself and your team as a unit, and your team members know themselves and their team as a unit, you already know and have managed the most dangerous situations you will meet.

Mock Forums

Prepare the groundwork by processing issues with your team members ahead of time. In San Francisco a few years ago, a mixed Asian group of Chinese, Korean, and Japanese people decided to hold an Open Forum to process issues of sadness and anger about how Japan hurt China and Korea during World War II. The Japanese group members worked on themselves ahead of time, exploring one-to-one relationship issues, and noticing the various polarities in their own group—polarities they planned to process in the Open Forum.

When the three groups got together for the actual forum, the situation was extremely tense. I clearly recall an amazing Korean woman who listened closely to the apologies made by the Japanese, but then, in the last moments of the meeting, when everything seemed to be coming together, spoke out bitterly about the Japanese attacks on Korea. She said clearly and bitterly, with sadness in her voice, that though she appreciated all the insights gained from the various sides, in her heart she knew she never would and never could forgive the Japanese, regardless of how apologetic they were today.

Then, to the amazement of the many people in that large hall, someone said something briefly in Japanese, whereupon every Japanese person present got up and threw herself and himself to the ground. Faces to the floor, they spoke out, admitting their guilt and promising they would never let it happen again. It was an awesome sight. The

Korean woman could not help herself any longer; she let go, and with many others, broke into an uncontrolled stream of tears.

The point is that the team needs to do its work, and if it does, genuine change is more likely to happen.

Innerwork: Processing Issues Ahead of Time

After all this discussion, finally we need to assess your preparation, including your fear and courage in doing an Open Forum. The following innerwork is designed to make you feel as able as possible to use the abilities at your disposal.

1. Consider an issue you would like to see addressed in an Open Forum. What is the topic at hand? What are some of the possible subsidiary issues that might arise? Who are your teammates?

2. Can you imagine the circumstances under which you might feel the shyest in the Open Forum you are imaging? Can you imagine the type of person at the Open Forum who might make you feel the shyest or most fearful? What are the key elements and attributes? Confrontation? Humiliation? Sorrow? Guilt?

3. Now imagine what that person might say and how she might behave. This can be difficult to do, but try it anyhow. Listen to her viewpoint. What is it? Does she say or imply that you know too little, are insignificant, are out of place, etc.?

4. When you are ready, imagine *being that person,* thinking her thoughts and even gesturing the way she gestures. Now, in your innerwork, make faces and gestures like she might make. Sit like she sits; speak to yourself as that person. Note the feeling of being that person. What does this feel like? As that person, what is your central message? Write it out.

5. Now let's go back to your position, and if you can, appreciate your viewpoint as well. Be as kind as you can be, and think about what you might say in return. Take your own side lovingly and listen to your message. Speak back; speak about your viewpoint. Write it out.

6. Imagine something or someone that can help you and your opponent come closer together. Let your unconscious mind create a resolution, something simple and immediate. Take a moment with this. Notice how this coming closer happens, and write down this resolution. Is it someone who appreciates and loves both sides? Is it someone standing on one side or another?

7. Recognize how the roles you just played (namely, that of yourself and your opponent) might be parts of a larger group process. Imagine the whole group processing these roles; perhaps two figures come forward to process these roles as others look on. Play them out in your imagination, even write out some of the statements made by both sides, and get to know these roles and the positions.

Encourage other members of your team to do this preparatory work. Sharing some of your responses to the above questions with them can be an amazing way of rediscovering the depths of your friends.

Your personal innerwork is important for your own development and, at the same time, your innerwork is a political act—and it is not just yours. Your inner process with the conflict that made you afraid may actually turn out to be part of the group process.

Things to Remember

1. Even if only one person in one hundred is aware of what is happening, the group will feel safe, and respected.

2. Today you may look troubled or nuts. Tomorrow, it could be me. Therefore, "You today, me tomorrow" is my motto.

3. After discovering your personal goals, you need to ask the community members about their goals. Are they interested in feeling safer? Do they want a greater sense of community? What are the diversity issues? The economic issues? Know the history of the topic and the history of the people involved.

4. Any given organizational issue is a crucial label, because it is the one troubling your group just now. At the same time, the label is an umbrella covering subsidiary issues that are intimately connected to the issue being discussed. You need to know the subsidiary issues; otherwise, they will arise and detract from the main issue.

5. Now that you know your umbrella topic and its subsidiary issues, name your Open Forum. If you want to hold a meeting with all relevant groups present, it is best to choose a name for the forum that is inclusive, not exclusive.

6. Speak with the trusted elders of the groups involved on various sides of the issue. Elders are not just the bosses; they are folks, young or old, who are respected by their communities. Consider inviting the elders to sit with the facilitators.

7. Location and timing for the conference make a difference. Choose a location and a time that foster inclusiveness.

8. Advertising is important. Create a warm invitation, friendly and personal. In addition, do your legwork—call people and ask them to come. Make sure they feel respected.

9. To feel more prepared, find out from your friends, acquaintances, and co-workers how you are seen publicly in terms of your race, gender, age, education, etc.

10. Choose speakers from the most extreme positions you can find on the issue, to avoid the "hovering ghosts" phenomenon.

11. Conduct mock forums: Prepare to work on issues ahead of time, both in yourself and with teammates.

12. Work on your own feelings about the forum, and hold a mock forum inside of yourself, as part of your inner "worldwork."

CHAPTER 4

The Facilitator's Awareness Work

Now I am going to assume that you have laid the groundwork, conducted the mock forum, and arrived at the location where the Open Forum will be held. Good luck! There you are, standing in front of a group of people with or without a team of helpers, and you are about to begin. Now use your awareness and remember where you are. The dance is about to begin.

Introductions at the Forum

Take a minute to acknowledge the location you have chosen. Say something about why you chose this location, this area, this section of the city or countryside, board room or living room. Then it might be useful to acknowledge the language you are using. I use mainstream American English and am often unaware of how this marginalizes folks who have other English speaking styles or other first languages. Being an American citizen has many advantages, but a disadvantage is unconsciousness of the use of the English language. I have to remember my

U.S. accent when I am in the United Kingdom or Australia. In any case, mention something about your particular language and the other languages spoken by those attending the forum.

In the beginning, most forum facilitators are nervous because they are trying to forget that they are being observed, pondered, and evaluated by an audience full of people. Don't do that; remain aware of the scrutiny you are feeling and talk about the kind of person you are and the things you have learned from your life. Begin by introducing yourself; comment about your personality and communication style, admit the funny things about yourself, your fears, etc. Is your style emotional, or detached? Are you the type of person who is cool and self-certain, or nervous and self-critical?

If you don't speak about yourself right off the bat (if you do, keep it brief!), your audience will interrogate or even attack you at a later point to find out who you are. If you describe and explain yourself, they will not spend half the time trying to figure you out.

Depending on our location, Amy and I often describe ourselves as being white, essentially heterosexual, middle-class, U.S. citizens. Amy admits she is from the Midwest, nervous or excited. I confess I sometimes act cooler than I feel, and add something about our particular social standing, and its limitations or advantages, depending on the nature of the forum.

The point is to make it easy for your listener. Set the stage for being human! The root of the word *facilitate* is *facile*, which means *making things easy*. Tell them about your one-sidedness and your style. Amy always says, "Hopefully I have many styles, but often I feel shy and sensitive." Once, in a good mood, I heard myself say, "I am a white, balding male, aged fifty-nine, with this experience or that, a therapist with a bundle of unworked-out problems! In fact, I may be part of the very group you are eventually hoping to awaken."

A cab driver taking us to a conference in Washington, D.C., once told me the following joke. If in the years to come, you want to have a U.S. zoo with all the possible animals in it, better put a white male in that zoo now, because he is becoming an endangered species.

If you don't speak about yourself and your position, people will eventually make you aware of it, whether you like it or not. Of course, you don't have to say everything about yourself. In fact, it may be risky to do so. For example, in most parts of the world, it is still dangerous to speak about your sexual orientation if you are gay. Nevertheless, the more you say, the more people feel that you are leveling with them and are therefore trustworthy.

Who Is Attending?

Make a note about who is attending the forum, mention your awareness of other peoples, languages, ethnicity, sexual orientations, education, health issues, races, religions, etc. Then thank the people for having taken the time to come. You might consider the possibility that the number of people present is the right number. If that number is small, then what will happen could only happen in a small group. Small groups are really important, because with good facilitation, very close relationships can be seeded, and a core group of change agents forms.

If the number is large, then you can assume everyone is needed to make an organization-wide change. You may want to mention that those who did not make it to the meeting are present anyhow and will eventually also be represented by you or others during the forum. (I'll talk about how to do that later.)

Recognize suffering. Especially in tense conflict zones where there has been a lot of injury and loss, acknowledge the enormity of the undertaking: Say something like, "We are going to do an Open Forum on an issue that is very painful. Some people may not want to think about this issue, much less discuss it. That is why not everyone is here. Thanks to those of you who have come."

The pain of the issues at hand traumatizes people, and no one willingly wants more of that. Many of the participants may be relieved if you merely note that there has been great suffering and loss. An optimistic, happy-go-lucky facilitator walking into an area where there has been much bloodshed is not appropriate or effective. If you ignore the trauma and history there, people will not trust you. They will give you a chance if you acknowledge that it is difficult to begin a discussion on such a painful issue. Make sure people realize that you empathize with them.

Thank the elders. Remember to pay attention to the governing deities. Show respect for the elders in each of the represented communities. Publicly thank them for coming. If they feel respected, those elders are more likely to return to their communities after the forum and carry on the work when you are long gone.

Native communities worldwide have reminded us of ancient rituals that honor the elders (and everyone else as well). Honoring the elders may be a way of honoring the history, ancestors, and spirits behind each group.

Thank your helpers. Be sure to warmly acknowledge those who did the background legwork involved in creating the Open Forum. Show the community who these people are. They are part of both the background and the foreground, as some may help you act out roles and share the job of facilitation with you up in the front. You need to remember that in thanking these people, you are also asking them (and everyone) for help; what needs to happen depends on everyone.

The obvious facilitators stand at the front, yet many others can ably facilitate the whole process from any position in the room. In fact, those on the "sidelines" can be as helpful or sometimes even more helpful than the identified facilitators who get the most focus. If you don't know what to do in the midst of the forum, you can always look for help from your team members. If they have their hands raised, ask them to help facilitate. Their "sideline" comments about the atmosphere in the room, such as "Lots of pain in this room," or "Feels like relief has happened," can be turning points for everyone.

Clarify the timing. How you deal with timing in an Open Forum depends on your style and the culture in which you are working. If you don't mention the time that has been set aside for your location, and for the Open Forum, people may start leaving in the middle. If you say, "This is an Open Forum that is scheduled from 7 to 9:30 P.M.," chances are great that people will stay till the end.

Limit speakers' time. When cultures were smaller and more monolithic, and when people did not have to get up the next morning to go to work, all-night sessions were feasible. Today, people in most cosmopolitan settings leave after a given amount of time. Therefore, timing the invited speakers is important, since you want as many people as possible to speak during the evening.

I think limiting the invited speakers to five minutes is helpful.

"Experts," politicians, and social activists may want to go on forever, inadvertently dominating others by speaking on and on. Don't worry about cutting them short. Such speakers may not feel hurt if you tell them the time limitation ahead of the event, then, at a given moment during their presentation, smile and say, "Your time is about up!"

So hold the experts to five minutes—five minutes initially, then two. After the first fifteen or twenty minutes, when the first three or four introductory speakers have told their stories, the moment has come to let everyone speak. Process-oriented Open Forums do not depend on asking people to speak who have prepared speeches, but rather they focus on the dialogue between individuals. Therefore, it is helpful to ask audience members to voice their views as briefly as possible. In large Open Forums, holding folks down to about two minutes each by saying, "Your two minutes are up," allows others to speak as well. You can frame your request positively by saying, "Yours is an important point, now sum it up, please, because others are waiting to make points as well."

As I said, facilitation means "making things easier" for the community, so timing speakers is facilitative in that it favors the whole community. However, you must be careful about how you do this. Simultaneously, you need to communicate respect for the individual (the part) and the community (the whole).

Beginning facilitators often feel too shy to say anything, fearing that their interventions will harm or offend someone. I don't support this kind of shyness because it leaves the community open to abuse by powerful individuals. Protect the public, while respecting the speakers. In ongoing organizational processes, the group itself will eventually take over the role of facilitator and tell people when to stop. However, in an Open Forum lasting only a short length of time, the community depends on you to establish and hold the parameters.

Mention your goals for the forum. For example, one of my goals is that the community gets to know its various parts. Communities are rarely aware of their diversity issues, strange as that may seem, until each diverse issue is voiced in the forum.

Another central goal is safety in the community forum. Safety has as many meanings as there are people in the forum. People feel unsafe if they are not able to defend themselves against others who dominate the communication channels. Ongoing communities need to come to a consensus on what safety means and how it helps some but may impede the voice of others. The topic of safety is always connected to *consciousness of abuse,* not just in the overt social sense of one person or group using power to hurt another, but in the covert sense of one person or group using a style that obliterates others.

People with nonmainstream types of communication styles often feel unsafe in speaking publicly. Shy people don't feel safe. Some women don't feel safe when powerful men speak. Some men are afraid of powerful women. It's not safe for people of one race (or gender, or religion, or sexual orientation, etc.) to speak if they are only part of a small percentage of the people present. Often when someone from a minority finally speaks in an Open Forum, mainstream people have difficulty understanding them either because those in the minority are too nervous and rattled to be clear, or because they have become terrifying and bitter for having been repressed so long. (In the latter case, overpowering behavior may be overcompensation for their fear of reprisal.)

Safety in an Open Forum is a matter of *your* awareness and community consciousness. The more you communicate awareness of processes, the safer people will feel. For example, if a person or a group threatens another group or individual, instead of only tolerating a silence, you might say, "In the moment, someone has spoken strongly, and someone else in the room might be too scared to speak back."

Follow Nature

You probably have various styles of facilitating. At any one moment you may be prompted from within yourself or from what has just been said in the forum to transform into a social activist who must change the whole world and wake everyone up to a given topic. Alternatively, you may be a savior and strive to save everyone. At other times, you will find yourself becoming a rug on which people can sit and chat. A rug simply creates atmosphere. You might have a more spiritual orientation and consider that your work is to follow the natural unfolding of human processes from moment to moment. This latter style is the one I like the most, though I may use the other styles at one point or another as well.

The spiritual attitude makes everything you do in life "awareness work." Whether you are gardening, washing dishes, driving your car, or facilitating an Open Forum, awareness attends equally to the signals and events. In awareness work, the most divine thing is exactly what is happening right now, in the moment, inside of you and in front of your nose. From the awareness viewpoint, change is inherent in all life; you don't have to work at it, change brings itself about. Noticing things can be easy.

If you notice change, change happens. You need awareness, not power, to notice and follow the unceasing flow of change. From the awareness viewpoint, what people identify with is being shown, and also what they do not identify with. You might notice that while an agreement or other kind of settlement is being arranged, some people are smiling but looking down. They identify with smiling but do not identify with the reason they are looking down at the floor. If you use your awareness and notice their depressed faces, despite their smiles, you know the time for settlement is not yet here for them and that they will not follow the settlement later. Awareness suggests you wait for another meeting. Another few meetings at this point can avoid decades of struggle and war later. Use your awareness to make change happen the most quickly.

Let's assume, then, that though others give you and your team various jobs to do, you see your basic task as a facilitator to be awareness work. Let's assume that you agree to follow the nature of things, the Tao. However, what is that Tao, the path of nature? It used to mean following the wind, listening to the call of the birds, the sounds of the forest, the rising of the sun, the sound of the owl.

What does it mean follow nature in an Open Forum? In previous books, I have discussed a number of elements that require awareness.

I have spoken of "weather reporting," that is, noticing and announcing the atmosphere in the room. Keep your eye on body signals, such as the smiles, postures, and gestures that do not make immediate sense to you.

Notice roles (the momentary players, such as the "oppressor," the "oppressed," "terrorists," "leaders," etc.—each group has its own names for these roles).

You will need to become aware of "ghost roles"—that is, people and events that are mentioned but not present or represented. (Examples of ghost roles abound: folks who have been spoken about but who have died, the trees spoken of in a discussion about the environment but not represented, or the president of a country mentioned who is not present.)

Notice communication barriers or "edges"—the sudden inability of individuals to speak or complete what they are saying.

Hot spots are especially important in the Open Forum. A hot spot is a moment during a group process where something flickers in the group's attention but is dropped because it is too scary, too emotional. You can find more about hot spots in my books *Sitting in the Fire* and *The Leader as Martial Artist*.

Hot Spots—To Cook or Not to Cook

There is no one fixed definition of a hot spot, since it is a matter of opinion as to what is "hot." For example, if someone mentions sex and everyone giggles, that could be a hot spot. If someone insinuates that the community has a problem that is difficult to speak about, then everyone is silent, that could be a hot spot. If men's rights at home are mentioned in Japan and everyone laughs, that is a hot spot. Facilitators of Open Forums need to develop awareness of hot spots.

In principle, hot spots contain core, essential feelings and are good energy in which to "cook" community issues. However, these hot spots are often so hot, at first, that the issues are avoided. Eventually you must explore them, because they are the places where fires and earthquakes can break out later. In geology, hot spots are places in the upper crust of the Earth where hot stuff from below touches the surface. They are spots where volcanic eruptions originate later.

In any case, after the first speakers have introduced the various sides of the topic to be discussed, use your awareness to notice roles, ghost roles, edges, and hot spots. Hot spots are important because they contain deep issues. If you miss a hot spot, it returns—and when it returns, it usually is in an escalated fashion. Most violence occurs because hot spots were never addressed in the first place.

For example, in the midst of an argument within a mainly black community in the United States where whites were being criticized for crimes done in the past, an African American speaker got up and pitted herself against the prevailing political mood by saying: "I am going to upset some of you. Believe me, God is not black or white or any other color." She was implying that being close to God could ameliorate the prevailing tense political atmosphere. However, her statement did the opposite: she created a hot spot.

At that moment, no one could focus on what she had said and moved on as if she had not spoken. Later, the topic of what it means to be black or white came back again, this time much more vehemently. A male activist corrected another woman speaker who had just said she felt she was not simply black since her mother was Irish and her father African. The activist said, "Remember, lady, as far as this world is concerned, you were born black, brought up black, and will die black." By this time, however, the hot spot had turned into a near-fiery inferno, in part because the community had not been able to explore the hot spot in the first place—that is, the conflict between the political and spiritual dimensions of being a person of color.

In Open Forums, give gentle attention to hot spots. Sometimes all you need to say is "Oops, that was a very big topic. Do we want to stay with it or move on?" In ongoing groups, the members develop a certain tolerance for the heat. However, a beginning group, such as an Open Forum, may not yet be ready to go into depth, that is, into all its hot spots. Participants need time. That is why most new groups usually want to forget hot spots at first! In contrast, large ongoing groups need little encouragement to enter hot spots. Open Forums, which have a more linear, safer, and mainstream nature, require gentler suggestions regarding the hot spot.

Let the community direct the situation. You could say, "Okay, now the community is veering away from an emotional moment. I just want you to note that some people may have a lot of emotions left over that weren't brought out in the moment, but apparently we have agreed as a community, as a whole, to go on, for the moment."

Alternatively: "This community wants to work on that hot spot, though others might be shocked by it. This may be hard for those who are shy about strong emotional experiences, but let's do our best together." The point is to recognize and acknowledge the diversity of issues and attitudes about emotions. "Is it okay with you folks if emotional stuff comes up? It may be useful, so hang in there, it may be better for all."

Of course, there are always people who hate any emotion at all, and in spite of the fact that you have advertised this as potentially emotional work, they are shocked to be exposed to the expression of emotion. What then? In ongoing community processes, they can be understood as a part of the community that needs to be represented, perhaps as a role that is afraid of hurt and harm. Try to bring them in *as a role, as players* demonstrating a fearfulness of the issues at hand.

Fearfulness wants to be heard. Just as activists may override fear, fear can also prevent the exploration of the issues at hand. The important thing is not so much what you say, but *how you feel* about the various roles such as fear. Being a facilitator often means walking the narrow path between the activist who wants progress and the shy person who wants to retreat.

Your Attitudes toward Microphones

Your attitude toward hot spots and toward the participants of the Open Forum shows up in many ways. If you are interested in the group's self-awareness, then in your imagination each part is crucial. Such an imagination can manifest in the manner in which you set up the room. For me, arranging an Open Forum in a circlelike fashion is crucial because it implies that all parts of the forum are significant. Sitting in the circle gives everyone the sense of being equally important.

In large groups, the location, setup, and use of the microphone are important issues. People with mikes have a lot of power; the question is how to use this power for the benefit of the community.

I prefer to place the mikes at different quadrants in the circle and keep the center open. If you place the mike in the center of the room for people to come and speak into, it encourages a few people to take over, but terrifies most from coming forward. When people can speak from the periphery, in a way, everybody becomes central. In a large group, several concentric circles may emerge.

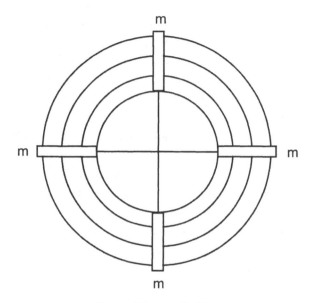

Open Forum Setting:
People are seated in concentric circles:
"m" indicates placement of microphones.

In very large groups, this setting becomes an aspect of the facilitation. Co-workers position themselves to hold the microphones and go around to different people. Then, if there is a debate on different issues, co-workers can help facilitate by interacting with a potential speaker, by asking her or him, "Are you sure you want to talk on this side of the identified topic?" If they don't do this, folks take the chance to gang up against one side of an issue. Co-workers can help ensure that every side is represented and has a chance to speak.

At some point in the beginning, explain to the participants that you and your co-workers want people from all sides to speak. Facilitation is a political act, and the relationship between co-workers is a political statement. For example, the way in which Amy and I relate to one another when we work together—or the manner in which we relate to other co-workers—conveys information about our understanding of relationship, gender, sexism, heterosexism, racism, etc.

If you are used to large worldwork groups where people speak up spontaneously, often without any microphones, you might rebel against the use of mikes and the semilinear manner they impose. However, in an Open Forum comprising hundreds of people, with a short period of time allotted, a focused style can be helpful to everyone, especially to those sections and positions in the community that may be shy to speak up otherwise.

So, help the community as a whole, and the mike-holders in particular, to focus on the issues and let others speak as well. Once community members know themselves and their collective hot spots, they can better tolerate the emotional experiences in the background. In time, ongoing community members will work together, becoming a self-organizing awareness process that directs itself, making the original designated facilitators nothing more than remains from the past. Becoming an almost irrelevant figure—enabling the organization to follow itself without you—hopefully is one of your goals.

Notice Ghost Roles

Before going deeply into events, you must respect the community's stated goal, the members' vision, and the job they want you to do. Respecting a community's style and goals is like respecting their conscious mind. If you have shown respect for that mind, it is usually going to be more open to going into events and experiences that are further from consciousness. What are these events and experiences?

The ones closest to everyone's awareness are ghost roles. Recall the ghosts—those people or events mentioned but not directly represented. Some typical ghosts can be found in the gossip of the day, especially when it concerns conflict, stealing, abuse issues, competitiveness, secret relationships, fear, and jealousy of other organizations. A typical ghost is usually the identified monster in the organization or town—the "she," "he," or "they" who purposefully or inadvertently overrides everyone else. If that monster is not present in the room as it is being spoken about, play it out, discuss how it may be present inside of everyone.

In open city forums, individuals and organizations easily get to the "edge" of what they feel can be said. Ghosts and edges are what make hot spots so secretive, compelling, and volatile. Hot spots are locations for an organization's unconsciousness, so how well an organization deals with hot spots will determine its future.

For example, in an Open Forum on racism, the overt racist often becomes a "ghost role," as are the "government leaders," with their horrid ways, especially if there are no government officials present. For example, in a recent Open Forum in Washington, D.C., many were speaking about the insensitivity of the government to the needs of the people. The government was the forum's "resident ghost," so to speak, perceived as not being present in the moment.

With awareness, you can help identify ghosts roles such as the government by pointing out that the ghost role of government is not just "out there," in the form of an external reality, but it is also an inner reality right here and now. You might point out that government argues its case polemically, using rational debate and political discourse that seems addicted to controversy. Such a "government" seems uninterested in the real betterment of all who are present. The government is that attitude in the room now that is not interested in the views of others! You might want to act out the ghost, saying, for example, "I am the government or the president. Since I am here right now, I want to tell all of you that . . ." How you deal with ghost roles depends on your personal style and the openness of the group.

Awareness insights about such ghost roles and hot spots serve as powerful interventions and are best delivered with gentleness. Remember that awareness itself can be used as a power tactic over others. Mention what you notice; call it simply a viewpoint, not a fact. For example, say something like "It seems to me as if the government might be an unrepresented figure."

Suggest an awareness intervention three times and if it is not picked up, recognize that it may not yet be "time" for the community as a whole to use that intervention. For example, if no one seems interested or able to go deeper into the government ghost, take your awareness as a suggestion to yourself and become aware of your own governmental attitudes. Tell the folks, "Whoops, that must be my process. I'll notice the government appearing in the way I speak."

Your awareness interventions either work or do not work, not because they are right or wrong, but because of the *timing*. You might think you see the key to everything and therefore cannot wait to enlighten others. Yet, to your puzzlement and dismay, no one listens. This does not mean you are not right; it simply means the timing is not quite there. Wait a few minutes, and the same statement may work—or it may not.

When working in an Open Forum, I try not to use "shop talk," terms such as "edges," "hot spots," "ghost roles," etc. Displaying your education and your facility with language is a kind of political statement. I prefer a politics that uses ordinary language. In Open Forums, technical language is not the point; the essence of the message is the point. That essence is one of open communication in a world that is interested in everyone.

For example, instead of using the term "hot spot," you might say, "That was an emotional moment, shall we return to it?" Instead of "ghost role," you might say, "That government is part of us right now in our attitudes."

I remember working with a group in a mental health center that was having trouble with their "boss." They said that the boss was a "real dictator" who had no feeling for others. Since the boss did not show up at the meeting arranged to settle the problem, the boss became a ghost role. Seeing that, Amy suggested that everyone play the boss. Suddenly, all the participants became more direct and straightforward; they became distant instead of behaving as usual—feeling and relating to one another. Gradually, each gleaned a different view of the boss and everyone laughed. The boss's style was just what was needed. In this case, the mainstream power, the boss, was a ghost—and one that was needed!

Semilinear Style and Escalation

The use of a semilinear style can be helpful when escalation occurs, which means that people either get depressed and leave, or they get louder and threatening. If you use a semilinear style, try, after someone from one side of the issue has spoken, to help someone from the other side speak as well and not just cower in the background in fear. In a tense situation, even if no one's hand from the "other side" is raised, you might ask, "Would someone from the other side like to say any-thing?" If no one chooses to speak, you can leave your role as facilita-tor and say, "I will just take this role temporarily, since otherwise it will be left out."

Ongoing organizations and communities have their own manner of dealing with moments of extreme escalation. In an Open Forum, we have a temporary community consisting of all those who are present (and all the ghosts from the "outside" who are not). Knowing how to work with escalation in an Open Forum is important, because people often become irritated, depressed, afraid, or hopeless about conflict that is not resolved. You can model methods of getting past this threat-ening point.

Call the two imaginary positions in conflict A and B. Imagine posi-tion A says, "Woof, woof, woof!" and position B responds with "Meeeooowww!" Let's say A and B, dog and cat, are really stuck. No one is budging. Things are getting louder and louder and beginning to scare everyone. Violence is imminent. What next? Run for the hills?

No, sit in the fire! One way of working with this escalation is to walk over to B, stand next to that person, and try saying something like, "Indeed, our position is truly Meeeoow, but some of us also see the point of the Woof!" Move back to A and say, "Woof is for us the only way to go, but then, after hearing from you, some of us will admit that Meeoooww is not entirely foreign to us!"

By alternately aligning with both positions, a little part of B is hear-ing A and a little part of A is hearing B, although the people in those positions may not want to admit it in a given moment. As the facilita-tor, you can go from one side to the other and say, "Yes, some of us over here do hear a little bit of what you are saying, though the majority of us in this position do not agree with you." This increases the fluidity of the process because you give people a model for going over an *edge*. They don't want to admit that they agree, but in their hearts, they real-ly *do* agree. Sometimes participants will not show agreement with the other side because they fear being perceived by their own side as a traitor.

Can you recall your own behavior when caught in an argument? Your basic stance may be, "I don't agree!" Yet, if you are 100 percent honest with yourself, you notice that a small part of you actually does agree with the other side. None of us is only one role. We have the other in us as well, though it takes some time and effort to admit that.

All of this leads to the hottest topic, facilitating social change! Let's not face that hot spot yet, but wait until the next chapter.

Things to Remember

1. When you are about to begin the Open Forum, take a minute and acknowledge the location you have chosen and the language you are using and how it might marginalize some people.

2. Begin by introducing yourself; comment on your communication style and personality, the funny things about yourself, your fears, etc. If you don't speak about yourself right off the bat (but keep it *brief),* your audience will interrogate or even attack you at a later point.

3. Recognize the diversity and the number of people who have come, and thank them for doing so.

4. Recognize suffering. Especially in tense conflict zones where there has been a lot of injury and loss, you need to acknowledge the enormity of the undertaking. Say something like, "We are going to do an Open Forum on an issue that is very painful. Some people may not want to think about this issue, much less discuss it. That is why not everyone is here. Thanks to those of you who have come."

5. Thank elders and all others for coming, and thank your helpers. Mention the amount of time allotted for the forum and keep invited speakers to five minutes, everyone else to two. In addition, be brief yourself! Mention your goals, such as safety and respect for all. Keep in your awareness the largest goal, that community members get to know the community's various parts. Communities are rarely aware of their diversity issues, strange as that may seem.

6. Awareness work means noticing the weather (the momentary atmosphere reigning in a group), which comprises roles (the momentary players, such as "oppressor," the "oppressed," "terrorists," "leaders," etc.). Each group has its own names for these roles—ghost roles (roles mentioned but not occupied by anyone), edges (communication breaks), hot spots (apparently forbidden topics), and so forth. Be gentle in conveying your awareness; let the people and their processes show you how to proceed. Remember that everyone has all roles inside.

7. Suggest an awareness intervention only three times. If it is not picked up, recognize that it is not yet "time" for the community as a whole. Take your awareness, then, as a suggestion to yourself. Tell the folks, "Whoops, that's my process, I'll work on it at home."

8. During periods of escalation, try having one speaker at a time discuss the issue. If this does not work, remember the formula for dogs and cats: A in B, and B in A. A little part of B is hearing A and a little part of A is hearing B, although they may not want to admit it.

CHAPTER 5

Consciousness during Attack

Open Forums are places where everyone hopes to make a better world. Some want to find out how to do this. Others have plans they want to share. Still others hope to awaken someone or some group to the issues at hand. In the background are hopes for a more successful organization (business, school, agency, etc.), more consciousness about diversity, and an equal distribution of goods and justice. It should surprise no one that the Open Forum is often a hot oven in which the new ideas are cooked.

Use your awareness here carefully. Some ovens are not hot enough, while others overheat. As the facilitator, your job is to sit in the fire so that new ideas are cooked but not burned. You need just the right amount of heart and heat. Exactly what "right amount" means, however, is unpredictable. The methods of this chapter—framing and centeredness during attack—should help you keep your oven at the right temperature.

Why the Heat Rises

Many participants believe that the heat must be kept up so that their points are remembered. For example, nonmainstream groups often suggest that creating discomfort for the mainstream forwards awareness of minority issues. Many social activists know that once their points have been made, people with power and privilege will ignore these points if they are not kept "on the hook." Those with privilege inevitably retreat from accusations of wrongdoing or suggestions to awaken to the needs of those who are not privileged.

At one time or another, everyone in roles of social power is identified as such and accused of unconscious use of privilege. There is no way around it; in a way, examining differences is what democracy and psychology are all about. What happens? Usually, at first, those with privilege retreat from that identification to find breathing space. However, they cannot really retreat from their positions because, like it or not, they are in the role of carrying the organization's "everyday mind," identity and focus, just as the activists are in the role of the "marginalized mind," fighting for recognition.

This fateful confrontation between the two sides of the community mind—its primary identity and its marginalized parts—typically moves in time from stalemate, through conflict, to some greater sense of inclusiveness. The ones in power hold on to their power and avoid meetings, and the ones without power attempt to amass it from the rear, so to speak. They plot to force the issue, become frustrated, angry, then troublesome, and finally, outrageous and even terrifying. Depending on the situation and group, organizations can become so volatile that they disintegrate. Or they may re-create themselves out of the chaos.

You as a facilitator are better off if you have worked on the organization's conflicts within yourself; you are more likely to be helpful to the group. The obvious reason is that facilitation requires more than facilitation skills; it requires a lot of centeredness—that is, innerwork on how the different parts of this community are different parts of yourself searching for understanding, respect, and freedom.

Innerwork on Stalemated Conflict

If you are not working with a group at the moment, think about some organization that is now, or eventually could be, suffering from a conflict between the "leadership" and others (such as marginalized activists).

Imagine a confrontation between these two parties. Listen closely in your innerwork to what people are saying. First, what are the leaders saying?

Leaders: _____.

(For example, the leaders might be saying, "We are doing a good job, we mean well, and are fed up with constantly being attacked.")

What are the opponents (or the activists) suggesting?

Opponents: _____.

(For example, "You people want all the power and have no real interest in the life situations of people you have marginalized!")

Now look at these two statements and try to find the core, the essence, of each of the messages. What is the essence of the leaders' idea? Of the opponents' position?

Essence of the leaders' message: _____.

(For example, "We are good people, stop hurting us.")

Essence of the opponents' message: _____.

(For example, "We are protecting ourselves from you. We hate to be so tough, and might relax if you respected and valued us more.")

Why does each side have to become so dramatic? Can you feel that reason? The reason the leaders have become so dramatic is that:

_____.

(For example, they are afraid that the organization will fail.)

The activists are dramatic because: _____.

(For example, they feel ignored as people.)

Now let me ask you a truly inner-directed question about yourself. How are you leading your life in such a manner as to sometimes marginalize important parts of yourself? In what manner have you been marginalizing one of your own deepest aspects—which has therefore become more dramatic in its communication to you, than you care to admit? If you cannot answer this question immediately, think about the last dream you can recall. Who was in that dream? And what aspect of yourself might that person or those people represent?

Consider the possibility that you have unwittingly projected your own psychology onto that leadership, or that marginalized group. Are you not in some way like these two groups? Do you not have a conflict between your own inner leadership and your own inner opponent who is fighting for recognition and appreciation, for her life? How can you resolve the conflict within yourself?

After doing this work, you may feel able to understand the various sides of your community or organization well enough to stand for them. In this way, during the forum, you can help the marginalized group make its points heard and enable changes to be made. You are more likely to feel compassion for those in power and enable them to take a stand and, at the same time, remain open enough to the issues about privileges and powers to create possible solutions.

Years ago I remember working with the top manager of a large multinational corporation. The company was failing financially; it was in a serious slump. The employees were deeply unhappy and rebellious; some were even quitting their jobs. To make things worse for the boss, his wife was having an affair with one of the lower-ranking employees. Before doing a group process or Open Forum with the whole company, I decided to work on myself. As I was in the midst of parting with someone and creating a new relationship at that time, I had no problem finding all the various parts of this company within myself. I was the company, the boss, the wife, and the employees!

My innerwork led me to interview the manager privately. I thought to myself that the employee with whom his wife was having an affair was a sort of ghost role. Was the manager himself and the business in need of that role? I asked him what his wife found so attractive in that employee. The manager told me he did not want to know the details about what his wife was doing in her private time. I told him I understood—who wants to go more deeply into a difficult situation?—and changed the subject. However, suddenly feeling freer to explore his wife's affair, he confessed that she had told him that the other man was far more interested in romance and relaxation time than he was.

That was the beginning of the solution to the manager's personal and business problems. I suggested that the corporation focus on making their product more romantic and relaxed, and that the manager do the same with himself. The results were outstanding on all levels. The business itself become more relaxed and improved dramatically as it became more connected with what the public wanted. The employees were happier, and the manager's relationship with his wife improved as well!

When the Oppressor Becomes a Ghost

Changing those in power is not always the key to a resolution of problems. Sometimes even when groups become more inclusive, some members from a marginalized subgroup may continue to push for more change. In these circumstances, it is important to consider the possibility that the oppressor is not just a role filled by those who have organizational power. The oppressor may also be a ghost role pervading the *entire* atmosphere.

How can an oppressor be a ghost? The ghost of the oppressor we wish to restrain may no longer be outer figures only, but also inner experiences that manifest as communication styles that insensitively "oppress" people. Insensitivity is what mainstream groups are always accused of. Of course, in principle, from the beginning of the conflict, both victim and oppressor are *roles* and not just people. A role is *never* just one group or person. That is why we are all fated, at one time or another, to take responsibility for the changes in a given role that need to be made.

In any case, the oppressor role is "spirit in the air," the human tendency to ignore others. Democratic groups are not yet trained to notice the existence of roles and spirits. Today we all focus mainly on identifying individuals with their roles. We think the evil is that person or group outside of ourselves. This pattern of externalizing "evil" is an important phase of community evolution. Most of history is composed of revolutions against those who have abused their powers. However, the next steps in creating a deeper democracy require awareness of roles and timespirits as well as people. Roles are more accurately called "timespirits," collective roles that change over time. For example, the government leader is a timespirit because in one century such leaders were queens, kings, and chiefs while in the next they are elected officials. Timespirits remain, while their images change.

In other words, the evil one is filling the roles of a momentary and changing tendency. You can remove the person, but the role usually remains. Not yet realizing this, most of us are impressed when we locate the oppressor as an outer figure. This makes big news. *The crook, thief, criminal, and liar were caught!* Every day, new oppressors are identified and jailed! Hurrah! Nevertheless, their number is inexhaustible, in part because so few of us are aware of the oppressor as a ghost role present in *everyone's* behavior.

Until now, the marginalized group—let's call it B—has been complaining about group A, which has the power. Let's say A just does not, or cannot, realize that it oppresses through remaining ignorant of the needs of the others. Group B is saying *change, change, change.* Let's say that finally A changes a bit. Now, B calls for more change, and group A changes some more, fulfilling what B asked for to begin with.

You would think everything would be fine now. Nevertheless, there are many circumstances in which B continues to call for change. Finally, A balks, refusing to listen. A becomes irritated and afraid, and withdraws. A thinks, "Let me get out of this untenable situation where I can no longer defend myself from B. B reminds me of an irascible teenager!" A tries to leave the situation and plots revenge and gossip against B.

Now the situation escalates. The quieter A gets, the angrier B becomes and the more A thinks B has gone crazy. B becomes dangerous, and both A and B feel they are victims of one another. The world has turned to conflict; both A and B feel they are victims! In a world of victims, you, as the facilitator, must look elsewhere, outside the world—in the dreaming—for the abuser. The abuser is a "ghost": that is, a figure that represents the manner in which people communicate and become rigid and insensitive to the other side.

Dreaming and Levels of Consciousness

Using your awareness, seeing and playing out ghost roles can enable even the most stalemated dialogues to move forward. But to see ghost roles, you need to distinguish between levels of reality. Frame the issues that arise in the forum according to the level of reality to which they may apply.

For example, when working on oppression, at one point or another the oppressor is clearly an outer figure or group, but then at another point it is an inner, or Dreamland, figure that is a form of behavior. Finally, the oppressor can be an energy, a power inherent in these inner and outer figures.

Any given topic has at least three levels of consciousness associated with it. Let me summarize these levels:

Everyday reality, or consensus reality: This is the world people identify as being the real one. In an Open Forum, everyday reality is the world of people and events, figures and facts. You have the mainstream and marginalized sections of the population. Statistics and numbers are everyday reality. Systemic change occurs when people begin to discuss changes in the organization's structure or rules—its expression of consensus reality.

Dreamland: This is the world of body signals and of ghosts and roles that people rarely see as themselves, but project outside into the world as parties (which are, or are not present). Dreamland is a reality too, but not a consensual one. For example, an oppressive style of communication can be a ghost role, part of Dreamland projected onto oppressive individuals or groups. Heartfulness, even God, or the Earth can be roles to be played out in Dreamland. Game-playing is a crucial aspect of Dreamland that every organization needs to experience at one point or another.

Essence or common ground: This consists of basic energetic tendencies, deep, common universal principles and experiences— such as the striving for life, death, and immortality—that all human beings in this universe may likely share at one time or another. *Essence consciousness* is especially important for those who feel marginalized, because they are not interested in the polarizations of everyday life.

The reason for understanding and defining these levels is that if there is an unsolvable conflict at one level, you can always turn to another to find the resolution. If everyone is a victim in everyday reality, the oppressor can always be found in Dreamland—that is, in the body signals and unidentified and disowned behavior. In the case of A and B, the oppressor is in A's thoughts of retaliation and in B's unmitigated push for change.

Notice and "frame" the level that currently prevails. For example, in the moment that everyone is complaining about everyone else, you might discuss the sense of victimhood in the room and mention that the oppressor has disappeared out of sight and moved into Dreamland! Announce to everyone that dreaming is about to begin, and play out an abusive form of communication.

Frame your work as a *dreaming* and play out the dream world oppressors in plain sight. Dreaming is an important aspect of deep democracy. Instead of the tribal dances of old, in which folks danced the spirits of the environment, you can now "dance" the oppressor and the oppressed, in a sort of theater for all to consider.

Framing merely helps to clarify the picture of what is happening. Framing is a kind of art. Framing something as the dreaming is merely an awareness statement bringing into the open something that has been unseen until that moment. While playing out the dreaming, consider the work to be theater and get deeply into it. You may relieve many of the tensions due to unseen issues and enable things to move forward more easily. Augusto Boal, in his *Theatre of the Oppressed*, speaks in detail about how he expressed the world-views of Brazilians with psychologically oriented techniques used in theater to make change.

Hold in mind all levels of consciousness while dealing with any one of them. Frame the levels at which discussion is taking place; otherwise, the levels of consciousness war with one another. For example, when dealing with dreaming, remind everyone that you are dealing with only one level of consciousness in the organization, the dreaming level. Otherwise, someone will say, "Hey, there are real problems here; you can't dream now." Alternatively, while focusing on outer change at the everyday level, someone might say, "The way things are going is wrong; the method feels oppressive." This might be a call for more awareness of Dreamland. Frame things in terms of systemic change or Dreamland changes, depending on what is happening.

Remember the Umbrella

Each level needs the other to work. What's the sense of unity, essence, or common ground consciousness if it cannot help us to process the problems and issues of everyday reality? Framing things makes the diversity of methods and viewpoints more conscious and minimizes clashes between them.

There are many different aspects of organizations under the umbrella of any one given Open Forum topic. As I said in chapter 3, part of your preparation is familiarizing yourself with the various topics and how they are related to one another under any one given topic.

Sometimes aspects of an organization can be understood in terms of groupings. There are always at least three such groupings under the umbrella: (a) the entire organization, (b) interpersonal relationships among members, and (c) the psychology of individual members. All levels need focus for the organization to work well. For example, existing interpersonal problems may reflect problems in organizational structure. Sufficient time is rarely allotted for working out interpersonal relationship disputes in organizations. Parties are not enough!

Let's say that an interpersonal issue arises during an Open Forum discussion about a given topic. If the participants give you a consensus on putting aside the main issue and focusing on the interpersonal problem, you can frame that decision as follows: "Let's work on that issue in a few minutes and allow interpersonal issues to complete themselves first. We can return to the organizational issue later."

No one social or organizational problem can be solved at one level alone, and there is no such thing as a diversion from the main issue. Of course, in standard procedures, these apparently extraneous themes and issues are considered "out of order." However, a process-oriented facilitator knows that the resolution of any one topic requires considering all the topics and issues. How do you consider them all? Framing clarifies the flow of events in simple terms, placing situations in a framework that shows the different umbrellas, issues, and aspects of these issues.

For example, at the Open Forum on sexism mentioned earlier, a lesbian accused the mainstream, female facilitator of focusing only on relationships with men. "You are heterosexist," the lesbian said. The point is that the facilitator did not realize that homophobia and heterosexism are subsidiary topics under the umbrella of sexism and required mentioning to foster diversity consciousness. You can't deal with sexism without also framing—that is, talking about—racism and homophobia.

As different issues arise and are framed, ask the group: "We have various topics. Shall we finish one, then go to the next? Or shall we first work on this internal struggle within the women's community, then go back to the forum topic of sexism?" You will be able to know the answer by what people say or by the sounds in the room.

Recognizing Subgroup Conflicts

Members of a subgroup often conflict with one another during Open Forums because they have diverse methods of bringing their points across. You might frame that disharmony by saying, "That subgroup is now showing all of us how they work on themselves. Take them as a model of diversity."

Let's say that the middle-management employees seeking recognition from the bosses have a conflict among themselves. Alternatively, members of a minority group fighting for recognition and equal rights get into conflict with one another during an Open Forum or an ongoing community process. Whatever the particular identifiers of the subgroup in conflict, frame the intragroup discord as a crucial learning experience for everyone.

Imagine two people from a marginalized group fighting with one another, just as they are about to make their point to the larger organization. What a painful moment! As an Open Forum facilitator, you should be aware of various possible viewpoints toward marginalized groups getting into conflict when those with greater social powers are observing.

One viewpoint is that minority-group conflict occurs because all marginalized groups suffer from internalized oppression. There is truth to this viewpoint; each member of a marginalized group internalizes a sense of marginalization that she or he picks up from the mainstream. For example, many individuals who do not share the physical characteristics of northern Europeans (light-colored skin, eyes, and hair) feel something is wrong with their appearance. Internal conflict in any marginalized group is due, in part, to the internalized oppression of individuals thinking that the mainstream European appearance is the best.

Another viewpoint about conflict within marginalized groups is that it exists because people in mainstream groups are unaware of their privilege and do not support the marginalized community enough. Worse, those in power indirectly support intragroup conflict by feeling relieved when there is trouble amongst the "rebellious," for it takes the heat off the mainstream.

Still another viewpoint on this subject suggests that, in addition to the valid factors cited in these other viewpoints, the marginalized group needs to unify itself. I have also experienced that some marginalized groups rally around awareness work to create a tighter community. In essence, they say, "We're bored with thinking about the mainstream; let's work on ourselves. We are much more interesting!"

A group that works together is a group that can't be stopped. They have the power to accomplish the impossible not because of their stationary or harmonious unity, but because of their ability to model community by taking a fluid approach toward their own diversity.

Still another viewpoint on the internal conflicts of marginalized groups is that they are conflicting with themselves in part because the entire community has no model for how to conflict in a public setting. Marginalized groups have more experience and are often better at this than the mainstream sections of a large community.

Your Inner Process during Attack

Let's say that you have learned to frame issues and notice consciousness-level changes that occur under the umbrella. You feel prepared. However, there is something that does not easily fit under the umbrella of the Open Forum topic: personal attacks against you.

Though you probably do everything in your power to avoid being attacked, there seems to be no getting away from it. Such attacks may be inevitable, since, being human beings, facilitators inadvertently become one-sided, prompting an attack by someone or some subgroup of the community who feels forgotten. If you find yourself under attack, admitting your one-sidedness can create a quick and satisfactory solution. However, some attackers are not satisfied with quick solutions and you may be inadvertently pulled into a debate. What then?

In the first place, share with others how you see the situation. Perhaps you see what is happening in terms of modeling how someone with social power in a given context (such as yourself, as a facilitator) can transform and learn from what is happening. If you are part of a marginalized group yourself, you may see the situation in terms of mainstream values marginalizing a given community.

However you see the situation, if you cannot avoid it, get into it consciously. I suggest that you ask one of your co-workers to help facilitate that debate. Then, hold your breath, and enter into dialogue with the person who just attacked you. Ask the participants if it is permissible to do that, as long as your dialogue with the attacker does not last a long time. You might add that you hope this dialogue will be helpful for all, especially since your attacker's viewpoint and your viewpoint may be two of the central roles in the conflict field—roles that have not yet been sufficiently represented.

In this way, you may be helpful to the group, especially since your skills at conflict work may enable you to listen and communicate deeply, resolving issues in a way the group has not yet managed. Being publicly attacked is no fun, but it can be utilized in a way that benefits everyone.

Perhaps the attack occurred so quickly that the attacker was barely conscious of what occurred. If the attacker does not want to, or is not able to, enter a dialogue with you, you still have the option of doing innerwork, this time in public. This means showing your inner process to everyone. I suggest framing this first, saying something about how your inner process may be a model of the group process that has not yet occurred, bringing forward feelings that have not yet been expressed in the group.

I remember one courageous woman facilitating an Open Forum on women's issues in an organization. At one point, another woman indirectly criticized her. The facilitator asked the forum if she could focus on what she called her "inner critic" in public. She said nothing about the criticisms from the forum participant, but claimed only that she, as a facilitator, had to work on an inner problem between a critic and herself. The forum participants were stunned by the change of focus from the women's issues to a Dreamland theme. However, the way in which the facilitator managed to frame her request captured the attention of the participants. Everyone listened intently as she described herself as a very feeling person, while her critic was very logical.

To make the story short, the critic told her that she was worthless. Instead of just being depressed, the marginalized, "feeling" side of her spoke back, saying that feelings were valuable and crucial to all organizations. Her innerwork became a sort of teaching for all who were present. Better yet, she felt enthusiastic rather than depressed about the indirect attack. Her innerwork was clearly both personal and, at the same time, political.

Regaining Your Balance after an Attack

Everyone has their own methods of dealing with public attack, including repressing and trying to forget the insult. However, if awareness and community are your goal, if deep democracy and bringing the dreaming to life are important to you, then processing the relationship issue is the best way of regaining balance.

Recently someone criticized me during a large Open Forum, saying that though I said I was interested in individuals, she felt constantly ignored by me. The group had already decided to focus on an issue in which she was not interested. Nevertheless, she wanted to know why I went with the desires of the group and ignored her individual topic. Nothing I said seemed to help. So after asking Amy if she would facilitate the situation, and after having gained the group's permission to go into an exchange with her for a few minutes, I used my awareness and accepted the process trying to emerge.

I openly admitted I felt hurt by her public attack, and even admitted that I felt like crying. She held her own, insisting that I had ignored her. After she spoke, I went on, telling her that doing such Open Forums was no easy task, that I was frequently frightened. The more I spoke, the more I realized how much I appreciated her attacking me. After all, I had never revealed so much feeling or complained so bitterly before about how difficult large forums can be for me. I thanked her many times for bringing this part of me out.

I no longer remember the content of what she said, but I do recall that she was more than satisfied. In that moment, she and I moved closer, and we even hugged one another. I was very touched afterward when she privately apologized for attacking me in public. She explained that she had not realized how I had sacrificed myself for the situation.

She was right about several things. She had been marginalized by the overall group process, just as I marginalized my fears. Furthermore, the facilitator is a role, a kind of authority representing the whole group, and as such, can sometimes be used—sacrificed—by members of the group who feel marginalized in the forum as a whole. It is courageous and important for individuals to take a stand and have the chance to interact with the leaders, facilitators, and eventually with the group as a whole. If more groups allowed such interactions, there might be less violence everywhere.

Your Trance States

Occasionally, something occurs during an Open Forum that confuses you or even makes you feel absent-minded, as if you were "not quite there." There is nothing wrong with being absent, relaxing, and letting things slide. However, if you want to know more about trance states induced in public settings, consider the following possibilities.

One possibility: Trance states are really states of confusion due to two internal conflicting opinions about yourself. On the one hand you were criticized, and on the other, you want to defend yourself, but feel you shouldn't. The result is that the attack and defense fight against themselves inside yourself, while on the outside, nothing remains to be seen but someone in a kind of trance, with an absented-minded expression on her face.

Another possibility: The trance is trying to move you into a new level of consciousness. In this case, you should deepen your trance, feel into it. Allow yourself to feel detached from the emotional situation and the Open Forum. Such states can be the beginning of the feeling, "Life is okay; I am not needed all the time; the community itself knows best, in any case. I will come out of this state when and if I am needed."

Many situations send us into trance states, in part to reduce the drive we have to succeed. Deepening the experience of the trance can get you to the point where you look forward to what will happen, instead of trying to *create* what you think should occur.

Be Clear on Your Switching Roles

Being fluid with your own states of consciousness and using awareness in an Open Forum enables you to drop the conventional role of facilitator at any one moment and become something else. Switching roles is part of every human being's process! Do so *consciously*. If, at any one moment, you feel your concept of facilitator beginning to transform, then *frame* the situation and go with the transformation by changing roles.

I have already mentioned how you can switch from being a facilitator who is mainly interested in others, into the role of someone working inwardly on herself. Or you can step into any role and play it out in a forum, especially if no one else is. If role-switching happens for more than a minute, frame the situation and ask one of your co-workers to facilitate. Just say, for example, "I am stepping out of my facilitator role, and now I am stepping into the role of social activist. So-and-so, will you please be the facilitator?"

Alternatively, you may want to step into a role of the teacher and want to give a lesson. Say, "Okay, now as a teacher I want to say . . ." The point is that you and others are clear on when you switch roles. Without this clarity, someone from the audience can rightly accuse you of abusing your position to get a particular point across.

Others might say, "You can't step in and out of roles—after all, you are the facilitator." You can answer this by admitting that they are right, as far as everyday reality is concerned. However, when it comes to dreaming, anyone can be, and usually is, just about everything!

Framing things usually makes it easier for a group to accept your fluidity. Be sure to frame things *before* you do them. Then, if someone does not like the lesson you gave, they can attack the teacher role, and—luckily for you—not the facilitator herself.

Watch Out for Clapping

There is nothing more natural than clapping to show appreciation for someone making a good point in an Open Forum. Nevertheless, clapping is usually only good for the one who is being appreciated. The party against whom the point is being made always feels ganged up on. As a participant, I love to clap for the side that pleases me the most. Clapping is a political statement. Sometimes my clapping even has a touch of retaliation in it against the other side. You can clap in the hopes of destroying the other side.

However, as facilitator, be acutely aware of the delicacy of such moments; they are usually hot spots. The other side that is being put down by clapping will eventually seek revenge. In my experience, people who are put down remain quiet for an average of twenty minutes. Then comes their retaliation against the whole Open Forum: "This is a horrible place and nothing good was accomplished."

Therefore, when folks clap, frame it, saying, "While many appreciate what has just been said, I still remember the other side." Then you model awareness of all sides.

In the Silence

If there is a pause during an Open Forum, and no one says anything, enjoy the respite! Consider the following possibilities:

Perhaps everyone is just relaxing.

Perhaps an issue has been resolved, and the completed issue needs naming.

Perhaps everyone is afraid of going further.

Perhaps something unmentionable occurred? Hot spot!

Perhaps people are afraid of speaking out because they do not want to be hurt by the authorities after the Open Forum.

There are many kinds of silence. If the silence makes you uncomfortable, explore it inwardly, and perhaps aloud. If you suspect the group is at an edge, or near a hot spot

Go back to the last speaker, and try to remember her or his message.

Check out any double signals given by that person. Did her body say one thing and her words another? Did she speak of hope but look stooped and depressed?

Go back into that double signal and imagine what its essence might be. What was inside that depression? Was that fatigue?

Mention, for example: "What a mysterious smile you have on your face. I wonder if the essence of that smile might not have been a secret and forbidden sense of glee about what was happening?" Alternatively, "Is there a secret sense of detachment, or is it condescension?"

Whether you check out silences and go back to the previous speaker depends on your reading of the signals. If your reading is wrong, the other person's gestures will probably correct you. If you mean well, it is unlikely that the person will be insulted at a wrong reading. Remember to assert that you don't really know what the silence and double signal mean, but are merely searching for the next step in the work. Finally, perhaps the group's silence indicates that the proceedings are done! Frame that, and say, "It's time to relax!"

Community Immune Systems

Heartfelt moments in an Open Forum are welcomed by some but may be experienced by others as irritating diversions from the "real work," placating people instead of making concrete changes. Remember the young teenager who spoke out at a forum on sexism about how she had learned to love herself and her first period? Everyone was deeply touched.

A social activist might say, "Let's not just feel good together; remember the real problems out there." Framing such heartfelt moments can give value to them and to the next systemic change as well. Say, for example, that "although feeling states seem antagonistic to the dualistic social action scene, in reality, they are simply different levels of the same community work. Sweet moments give some courage to make social change."

Communities coming together, eating together, partying and dreaming together can better work at organizational change. If we think of a community as being like a body, then "dreaming together" can be considered its immune system—a system that resolves present problems and prevents other problems from occurring. Likewise, if I cut my hand, healing depends in part on my immune system.

Community problems are the same. The immediate problem—say, financial catastrophe, violence, anger, hopelessness, sexism, racism, or ageism—needs first aid, social action! However, the problem cannot be healed if the total immune system of the community is not working properly. Communities with high "immunity" respond to problems quickly because the people like one another. They have experienced something that has brought them together. Such businesses, schools, and organizations run smoothly.

Groups and organizations with a great deal of pain are saying that their overall immune systems are weak. With such groups and areas, it is particularly important to switch levels, use your awareness, go back and forth to the dreaming, and encourage individuals and organizations to be proud of themselves for addressing all levels of conflict. And perhaps remind them all that the body develops immunity by first getting sick. Then it develops antibodies that fight off future infections. In other words, problems are the fastest way to healing.

Things to Remember

1. A frame helps a picture stand out. Similarly, framing topics, issues, and levels of consciousness adds clarity to the proceedings. For example, frame the work as being focused in Dreamland; talk about oppressors as ghosts if the oppressor

does not see himself or herself as such. *Act out* the oppressors for the forum.

2. If members of a subgroup conflict with each other, frame that by saying, "Now that group is showing all of us how to create community. Take them as a model of diversity."

3. At any one moment, you may want to switch roles and leave the position of the facilitator. Do so consciously and tell others what you are doing.

4. If you get attacked, enter a dialogue with the individual who attacked you, and ask one of your co-workers to facilitate. This may be helpful for all, especially if your attacker's viewpoint and your viewpoint are two of the central roles in the conflict field— roles that have not yet been sufficiently represented. Being publicly attacked is no fun, but may it eventually be of benefit for all.

5. Watch out for clapping. However good the clapping may be for the one making the point, the party against whom the point is being made feels ganged up on.

6. Processing problems can be the best way for a community to create immunity to new problems. If moments of togetherness appear, cherish them, for they strengthen the community's immune system.

CHAPTER 6

Ending with Why You Began

Whether your Open Forum is the one and only, or the first in a series of such open discussions, it is hard to close. How can you say good-bye when you are just saying hello? Yet you must. Congratulations, you are almost done. It was amazing. People spoke whom you had never heard from before. Isn't the human race awesome, inexplicable, horrible, magnificent, scary, unpredictable, predictable, and lovable? Do you dislike them? Are you feeling excited about ending? Will you miss them?

The Open Forum has raised questions, made invisible parts of a community visible, and addressed conflicts that have been submerged. This visibility is a path to resolutions that can occur when a lot of conflict work has already been done. That is why the only reasonable goal for a first meeting—unless lots of work has already been done in that given group—is to bring up issues, discover submerged problems, and model solutions. But wait, you are not done yet.

We Have Ten Minutes Left

Frame and announce the ending. "We have ten minutes left, and we are just beginning to discover various aspects of ourselves. What has to happen next? Who has not spoken? Who will do what? Where and when will we do it?"

If you bring up things that need to happen and not leave them for the very last moment, many will be relieved. Don't forget the other themes and individuals under the umbrella that have not yet been mentioned. If you don't remember them, they will erupt at the last moment, like drowning victims trying to survive. Therefore, it is important to mention that you know these people have not spoken yet, ten minutes before the time is up. That gives them the chance to speak and does not marginalize their issues.

I remember working at a large Open Forum that was called to discuss a racial incident that had occurred in Eugene, Oregon. For an hour and a half we focused on African American issues, mentioned Asian and Hispanic interests, but neglected the pain of the few Muslim folks who were present and had also suffered from racism. In the last minute a Muslim made us aware of our unconsciousness. She was unnecessarily kind to us; she praised us, but was constructively critical about having to force her way in because we had inadvertently marginalized Muslim issues.

When ending, the central question to ask yourself is "Why did I begin?" Remember why you were interested in doing this Open Forum in the first place. What drew you to this job? What was the great dream that you had around large-group work?

If you tell the folks at the end about why you did this work, some of them will feel that a part of them has been mirrored. For example, I think to myself: What did I want? I hoped that the people who come will be stimulated to think about themselves and those with other viewpoints.

I find that whole communities are always surprised at the power of diversity that they have previously ignored. Make a statement about the community's evolving knowledge of diversity. Here are a few more suggestions:

Talk about the new awareness gained. At the end of the forum, you might say "Today, we discovered topics x, y, and z and have pointed out ways to go deeper. Just at the end, new things appeared, and they will surely be on the organization's agenda for future meetings." Remember to feed the mainstream part of the participants' minds that wants prescriptions. Reiterate suggestions that were articulated directly or indirectly.

Mention that solutions were suggested; someone suggested trying this and that. Another suggested something else. All these solutions are important. Now "draw" a circle around all the suggestions with a larger, encompassing statement such as, "However, the big thing is that we came closer to being a community."

Talk about what you have learned. "I notice that there are different facts that I learned here." Sum up the learning according to the levels of what you noticed. I notice that the following systemic changes may need to occur here. Perhaps there will be more times for Open Forums in the future. Remember all the organizational and systemic changes that need to occur. I notice that systemic change is needed, legal and economic change. (For example, "Our group needs new rules and regulations or a change in the old ones," or "Our group should connect with other groups to create interconnections," etc.) Who will work on that? Or you might say, "Let's think about what happened here and how it might apply to workplace ethics." (For example, a group will be created to monitor hurtful situations.)

Talk about the realm of Dreamland. You might say, "There is work to be done on inner oppression. This is invisible at first, but it is a crucial aspect to the entire work. Some of us spoke; others did not feel they could speak yet. Some silence is golden, and some is due to internalized oppression. Many of us will want to talk about that with our friends later."

Working on internal psychological issues is often new for people. A lot of people don't do this kind of self-reflection. Tell them how to do this in simple terms. Tell them to remember that they have an ongoing group process inside of themselves and that, in their dreams, they will find figures representing, for example, mainstream values, and other figures from marginalized cultures. Tell them to bring both parts out, to speak to both parts of themselves, to facilitate the "inner Open

Forums" going on all the time. Tell them that without an *inner* Open Forum, their bodies will suffer ongoing tension that is as tense as outer life. Long live Open Forums!

Talk about relationships and home life. How about more consciousness of diversity in all your one-to-one interactions? Tell your friends about the Open Forum, consider together how your relationships are influenced by differences in class and race, finances and sexual orientation, fear and courage. You might say, "How about doing more Open Forums in this school (or in the workplace, or in the city)?" Suggest doing an Open Forum at the next religious or family celebration. Instead of just having a family get-together, suggest holding an Open Forum on the issues of the family. How amazing that might be!

Set up a network. Near the end of the Open Forum, distribute handouts containing telephone numbers of people to call in the organization or city for further support. Include numbers for legal and civil rights help, and a contact number for people who might want personal support following the Open Forum. Communities tend to take care of themselves, but if the one you are working with doesn't, you might help after the forum or suggest individual helpers to care for people. You might say, "If you need help after this forum, or have questions, ask community members such as Joe, Sally, etc. Who else will help?"

Put yourself in the attendees' position. If you had questions about what you learned at an Open Forum, or personal questions about yourself, would it not be a good thing to have someone to speak to? Perhaps you and others—including forum workers—can sit in the corner of the room afterward and answer such questions. (I will consider innerwork for your team at the end of this chapter.)

Allow gossip. The most natural process at the end of a forum is for individuals to gossip about what has just happened. Groups form spontaneously. You can follow this process by asking or guessing about topics that will be discussed afterward and on the way home. Suggest that those who are interested in those topics meet briefly at the end of the forum in this or that corner of the room.

To guess, ahead of time, which groups need to meet, consider

The issues around hot spots

The need some participants may feel to speak personally with invited speakers in small groups

Interest groups who might produce a next Open Forum

You might suggest

"People who want to discuss a hot spot, please meet in this corner of the room."

"People who want to speak with speaker A, please meet in this other corner," and so on.

For example, we had invited a neo-Nazi to one Open Forum we held in Oregon, and there was a lot of buzz around that. People would not let that person speak in public and booed him down. However, as soon as the meeting ended, half the room gathered around him to find out what sorts of "evil things" he thought about. When the neo-Nazi went to a corner of the room, he was swamped with people interested in speaking and arguing with him.

Sometimes people want to meet in another corner and discuss your facilitation style, ask questions, make suggestions, and so forth. You will certainly be in that group, at least for a few minutes. If the issues are still boiling, sometimes it is good to say, "Those who want to continue to discuss these issues, please meet over there."

In an Open Forum with an ongoing organization, you might even recommend that someone take notes on what happened (as long as there will be no retaliation against anyone for what was said). Then collect and copy the notes and create a community paper called *Open Forum Notes*. I guarantee, everyone will read them. Better yet, publish it on the Internet or via e-mail.

Future collaboration. In large forums, two or more organizations frequently become interested in working together in the future. You may have suspected this interest from earlier research you did into the nature of the organization. You can now help this interest in collaboration evolve by setting up a framework for working together. Suggest ways of networking, create e-mail and telephone contacts. Suggest that organizations (or organizational parts) meet now in a corner of the room to discuss their common ground and how they may be "separate arms" on the same body.

Specific semilinear methods for working with the small groups after an Open Forum might be modeled after the World Café concept or Open Space technology. World Café might be good for small forums, where people sit at tables for four with a piece of paper for a tablecloth. After twenty minutes, three of the four switch to another table, sharing what they learned, and make more notes. After several switches, put the papers together and you have a record of discoveries. Open Space technology is similar. People create interest groups around the main theme. They then brainstorm on the topic of that interest group and collect their discoveries and resolutions on paper, collecting the papers afterward (Atlee 2001).

State of ending. In ending, describe where you are as a group. You might mention: "We are ending at a community edge; the next step will be to go over that, so more flow can happen. Some group members or subgroups have spoken, next time others will." Alternatively, you might say, "We are ending with an understanding and resolution." You might suggest: "We all have discovered we need more information and are ending with open questions. Who will take responsibility for getting the missing information and communicate it to all?" and so forth.

Follow-up forums. You can begin to plan for the next meeting by suggesting a time and place to meet. Announce that now, before saying good evening to everyone. If this first meeting uncovered the various sides of the problem, announce a possible theme for the second forum. For example, call it "What we can do to make things better." Suggest that the goal is to listen fully to what is really happening, and eventually to pose new and creative solutions to the issues at hand. Ask who will help contact local political and community leaders who could not attend this time.

Imagine a third Open Forum. This could explore "What have we done so far and where we can go from here?" At that third meeting, you can ask: "Should we stop here? Should we go on like this in small groups? Should we invite an even larger group or the whole community to the forum?"

At the end, remind people in business organizations and ongoing communities that everyone needs to feel safe. Ask those in power not to demote anyone because of what they have said here. Remind everyone that some individuals were speaking as if in roles, and may not want to be held personally accountable for the content of what they have said.

Compliment everyone for being present. After all, they have taken time for this; they may have been shy about coming. Perhaps they wanted to change the world. Remember individual psychology. Many people had to struggle with themselves to stand up and speak, to present their viewpoints. Under certain circumstances, some may have risked their jobs or even their lives to do so. Remember them now. Thank them. "Thanks to those of you who spoke and interacted. Your ability to speak about the topics at hand enables us all to move forward."

Make a list of the community's various groups and Open Forum methods, and support these. Thank these groups, and mention that the good things that have been done by the present forum were based in part on what their past work already accomplished. Suggest that they may (continue to) collaborate with one another in the future. Tell everyone how to get involved in these groups.

To bring closure, you might tell them, "We've talked enough, now let's rest, eat, or dance. I brought some cookies!" This is the deepest moment in process-oriented community work!

Being Thanked for Your Work

As you are leaving the Open Forum, if you are like most facilitators, you hope to be thanked for your work. Open Forums, however, are not like giving lectures or making speeches. If you did a really good job, the people will think *they* did it! Therefore, it is not unusual for a facilitator to be ignored by the participants at an Open Forum. Perhaps no one thanked you for your work. Of course, your co-workers will support you. However, perhaps few people thank you—just as few people thank the sun for coming out after a dreary day.

People appreciate the sun, but they feel that nature did the work, or that the community did the work. If they think that *they* did the work, be happy. Your work was successful in the Taoist view of things. In a larger sense, no one "does" anything, and no one needs to be thanked; the power of life itself is at work and in need of recognition.

Before leaving the theme of being thanked, let's consider one more possibility. Your needing to be thanked could be a role in that community. Perhaps they are not kind enough to one another. In that case, do not hesitate to stand up next time—if the situation presents itself and your awareness work reveals frustration—and say, "Damn you, folks, I worked hard. I spent late nights thinking about you, and I want to be thanked! Is there not one nice person around here?" That is the fastest way of getting to the ghost who is not willing to give anything to anyone!

Then summarize the results of the Open Forum for participants. These results typically include

Personal awakenings that cannot be measured

Changes at home with family and friends

Awareness of diversity issues and related topics

Changes in the community or organization (possibly better health, less violence, more financial stability)

New collaborations and forums

Your Innerwork after the Forum

After the forum ends, you and your team will have a lot to talk about. Create a time to sit together (or meet via e-mail) to consolidate learnings and clear up as many things between you as possible. Help one another on personal clearing, work on relationship issues that may have come up between you, debrief on what you learned at the forum, and make a list of changes in yourselves that you want to make for future forums. Use any form of innerwork and relationship work that helps, and/or try the following exercise.

Since the problems addressed in the forum are not just outside, but continue within your psyche afterward, part of facilitating an Open Forum involves completing it as a group process inside yourself—and with your teammates as a group during debriefing time—soon after the forum has finished. The following innerwork may be helpful.

1. Recall someone or some group from the Open Forum that amazed or upset you the most, for whatever reason. Let's focus on one such person that upset you. Choose one. Recall what she looked like and how she behaved. Make a note about her behavior. Was she too aggressive, loud, insensitive, etc.?

2. At least for a minute or two, imitate her, sit like her, act like her, and finally be her. Sit the way she might sit, and speak to yourself the way she might speak. Try to feel your way into her feelings, just a little bit. Try seeing things from her viewpoint, then take on her viewpoint.

3. What is meaningful and accurate about her viewpoint, her way of thinking? Don't you also sometimes think or feel this way, even a little, on rare occasions? Try to identify such occasions.

4. What are that person's gender, race, sexual orientation, age, health, nationality, economic class, and educational background? In what way do these social characteristics or designations play a role in the feelings you might have about her, and about this side of yourself that she represents? You need to ask yourself these questions, because some of your feelings and projections are linked to social issues. What social power and privileges does she have (or not have) that you do not have (or have)?

5. How might you use that behavior of hers, and that power of yours that you have projected on her? Perhaps you can even use that power represented by her in a new or better manner than she is using it. Make a note about how you would like to use this power in yourself.

6. Now imagine meeting this real person again and notice any changes in your feelings toward her, if any. Consider and imagine in what manner your relationship with her will now change. Will it be more direct, softer, have more understanding?

Sometimes the most difficult people in the Open Forum are not the participants, but members of your own staff. This should not surprise you, since the staff itself is but a mirror image of the whole world, and you find the problems outside in the staff, just as the problems in the world and the staff are also within you. In any case, if staff members conflict with one another, perhaps sharing this innerwork will resolve those conflicts and help everyone grow both independently and together as a team.

Things to Remember

1. Ten minutes before the end, say: "We have ten minutes left, and we are just beginning to discover various aspects of this organization. What has to happen next? Who has not spoken? Who will do what? Where and when will we do it?"

2. Don't forget to mention that you are aware of those groups and individuals who have not yet had a chance to speak. This acknowledgment gives them the chance to speak and ensures that their silence does not turn into vengeance against the group.

3. The central question for you around ending the Open Forum is "Why did you begin?" Why were you interested, what drew you to this job? Mention what the forum did and did not do. What was the great dream that you had around large-group work?

4. Make a statement about participants' evolving knowledge of diversity issues: "Today, we reaffirmed or discovered topics x, y, and z."

5. The linear part of the community wants prescriptions. If you have some, or if the Open Forum produced prescriptions, reiterate them. "This is what to do next." Also reiterate any organizational or systemic changes that need to be made. "I notice that systemic (legal, economic) change is needed. Who will work on that?" You might also say, "Let's think about what happened here and how it might apply to workplace ethics."

6. Talk about what you learned, summing things up according to the levels you noticed: "There is work to be done on inner oppression." Or you might say, "How about holding more Open Forums in your school (or workplace or city)?" Suggest to people that they create an Open Forum for the next religious or family celebration.

7. Post telephone numbers of people to call in the organization or city for further support. Provide contact numbers for further legal and civil rights help.

8. At the end of the forum, suggest meeting areas in the room to discuss things further, including the hot spots.

9. Announce a possible theme for the second forum; call it "What We Can Do to Make Things Better." The goal might be to listen more fully about what is really happening and eventually to pose solutions to the issue at hand.

10. In a third Open Forum, you might create a title such as, "What We Have Done So Far and Where We Can Go from Here."

11. Whenever you think about the Open Forum, remember that it is as much an innerwork project as an outer one. It's all about You, the community. That is the way to thank the Great Spirit.

A Second Revolution

CHAPTER 7

The Psychosocial Activist

In part 1 of this book, we prepared for the Open Forum and explored conducting and ending it. There were a number of awareness tips that were general enough to help you get through your first few forums. However, as you develop and relax as a facilitator, your ability to notice more about what is happening will increase. This second section deals with more advanced awareness tips and personal development.

Learning from Open Forums

Whenever I see myself or others doing large-group work of any sort, the activist in me is so thrilled that the new deep democracy paradigm is being tried that I stop thinking about what new things I might learn. After all, simply doing the work itself is an amazing experience and a learning one.

However, even the best of paradigms wear out quickly if it does not have some form of built-in learning procedure. The student in me who likes to learn new things wonders, "What could be done better?" Then I remember: Feedback is the teacher for a process student. The teachers of worldwork are the events themselves. If you have what the Islamic mystic Rumi calls an open or "guesthouse" attitude toward life, then events themselves are your teachers.

Since worldwork is diversity consciousness, I ask myself during and at the end of each meeting: How good was my consensus reality awareness of individuals and their issues? Was I aware of ghosts in dreaming? Have I learned about the organization's story and gained any insights into its dreaming, its emerging fairy tale?

Discover the Organization's (or City's) Story

Is the organization just learning about its ghosts and issues? Is it in the midst of a fairy tale filled with everyday problems, heroes, consciousness bringers, and activists? Now is the time to create a story from what I know. Perhaps some of the other participants or team members will help me formulate this story.

Just as individuals want to know their personal myths, organizations are looking for their evolving tale as well—that is, the expanded version of its everyday reality which includes every person, ghost, devil, and goblin. How are the issues tied together with jealousy and pain, love and God? I have not learned enough until I can tell the emerging story of an organization, until I can say something like the following:

> *Once upon a time, not long ago, there was an amazing city (or an organization) troubled by certain people, issues, and problems. Everyone was nervous and apprehensive. Some thought the situation was not bad, others were deeply troubled by events.*
>
> *Then one day, someone noticed or dreamed about a ghost in the forest, a ghost from the past or the future. A little girl, who had not yet learned that ghosts were scary, went out into the forest and spoke with the being. The ghost said, "Ah, you have forgotten me, your world does not realize I, too, am here. At least and at last you have discovered me. Tell the others the following message. I am here!"*
>
> *The child was thrilled with her new friend and brought the message back to the community. But many did not want to listen. Others wanted*

to ignore the ghost. But the girl said, "Just listening to the ghost would be helpful." To make the story short, a few people did listen, and this increased everyone's sense of community. Exactly what happened was . . .

Learn from events, put them together, and tell the story. You might even predict the future.

Discover Your Essence

In addition to learning from outer events, I feel I have not learned enough unless I have learned from my own behavior about who I *really* am, about my own essence. You don't know yourself until you study your own actions as facilitator and sense the essence of your behavior.

Let's say some of your actions or behavior as a facilitator attempt to change the world, save one group, overcome another group, or spread harmony, etc. Learning about the essence of your behavior means discovering its roots. What lies behind the outer action?

For example, we might guess that if you wanted to save one group against another, that the essence of your behavior was to spark consciousness in yourself and others, and create a sense of community and safety for all. If we learned from your behavior, and guessed its essence correctly, you would feel deeply understood.

The core or essence of your style (such as creating a home or community) is the dreaming root of who you are. Most of your behavior can be traced back to this essence. The essence of your particular style as a facilitator is what you give and bring to this world. People may forget your words, but they won't forget the essence of your energy. Your essence is what finally comes through to others, it's what works, regardless of the methods you learned.

You can learn worldwork, you can learn how to do an Open Forum, but you do all this best if you do it with the essence of your own individual style. So after every meeting, ask yourself about your style, and the root or core of this style. Don't change it, but live this essence consciously, identify with it. Are you a community maker, a bringer of justice, an angel in disguise, a revolutionary? Whatever your nature, be its student and its representative.

The Team as a Shaman

A next step in learning about large-group work is to think about your team and to reconsider the meaning of teamwork. As I have said several times in the first half of this book, your team picks up the vibes and mirrors the psychic atmosphere of the whole community. In a way, your team is something like a shaman who, by definition, takes on the disease of the patient and solves it within herself. The innerwork I presented at the end of chapter 6 should help in this "shamanic" work.

A conventional team metaphor is that of a group of people climbing a mountain. Each must support the next, otherwise everyone falls. If one person slips, all die. However, a worldwork team is different. Its goal is not getting to the top but *following nature*. The measure of success in worldwork is different.

Whereas conventional teams see a "slip" as a mistake, a worldwork team recognizes the slip as The Way—that is, as a manifestation of the Tao of the entire community. If the goal is awareness (including consciousness about diversity), then success is not measured in terms of reaching the top. Success can be redefined and experienced in relation to the degree of awareness of what is happening. If a "slip" happened, what can we learn from it?

When there is teamwork, members respect the differences between them. One might say, for example: "My co-worker would do this in that situation, but I prefer the following direction because of what I believe in. Perhaps we are both two roles in the present Open Forum field." Worldwork teams understand their own diversity not only as facts, but as roles that everyone can move in and out of.

Co-workers Modeling Solutions

If team members aim for awareness, what unfolds is going to always be a surprise. I have been amazed at the kinds of support my co-workers have given Amy and me in the midst of hot spots. I know that from the sides, I can sometimes see things to help the facilitator up front. However, I sometimes forget that the same is true when I am in the front.

During one large Open Forum, the group was working on racism in the inner city. An African American couple got up and said that when they complained to school authorities in their area about racism among the kids, the authorities refused to listen, saying that the problems were exaggerated. A tense discussion ensued in the forum about what to do with school systems. In the midst of the discussion, one of our team-mates came forward to model how to resolve things. She spoke about difficulties that she had, as the mother of an African American child, confronting her school system. What a help that mother (and team-mate) was in getting a stuck situation moving. Everyone was relieved.

Then, to my amazement, even more help arrived! Two other team-mates came to the center of the room and role-played a hypothetical dialogue with the school system. In front of everyone, they showed just what needed to be said to get things rolling throughout the school systems in that state.

The role-play of our friends gave practical suggestions to concerned parents and everyone about how to interact with that apparently insensitive school system. In addition, they turned the stalemated situation with school authorities into a creative and achievable task.

The Intellectual's "-isms"

At every forum, there always seems to be someone who takes the role of the "cool intellectual expert." This person typically insults everyone who is upset by the situation by looking down on their feelings and implying that they were unable to simply understand "the facts." They might even say, "It is all a matter of intellectual awakening!" This attitude irritates most folks and creates conflicts at many levels. First, there is a conflict of style between intellectual and emotional participants, then, second, there may be a conflict between cultural styles of expressing viewpoints.

I remember one Open Forum on racism in which a man spoke about having risked his life to protect people against abuse by racist skinheads. Police, trying to keep the conflict with the skinheads in hand, inadvertently injured the man now speaking at the forum. A woman stepped forward and coolly dismissed the man's suffering, telling him he should have understood the police were just doing their job. In her mind, the man hurt by the police should not complain about them or the skinheads, but think instead about the definition of the word "racism."

Quoting from a dictionary, she quietly read: "Racism is a belief that race is the primary determinant of human traits and capacities and that racial differences produce an inherent superiority of a particular race." Her academic tone marginalized all the feeling into the periphery. While the man was suffering in the corner, the intellectual drew her dry conclusion: "In a free country you must be free to dislike and discriminate. Look—it says so in the dictionary."

One of the African American facilitators stepped forward, reacting strongly to her coolness. The intellectual froze on the spot. To balance things, a white teammate of the African American took the side of the intellectual, who was no longer able to speak, and spoke for her. The three people—that is, the two facilitators and the intellectual—debated in the center of the room. The facilitators represented the two roles in conflict, the social activist and the intellectual, while the woman who loved the dictionary stood next to the facilitator on her side.

The intellectual role said, "Let me speak, I have a lot to teach!" The other side (for whom the audience was cheering) said, "No, your approach is marginalizing and hurting us. You are acting superior yourself!" The intellectual side insisted that clarity is the point. The activists did not agree. Those in that role said clarity is a particular mainstream style that may be valuable under some circumstances, but is disrespectful of the suffering of those in minority positions.

The interaction between the facilitators playing both roles resolved things, and a momentary understanding occurred. Seeing two facilitators resolve an issue for the rest of a community was awesome. They framed the conflict as a divergence in approaches. This addressed the sense of superiority that emanated from the intellectual. A more complete perspective on this interaction might see the adversaries as working on a global conflict between different economic classes. Emotional coolness is generally accepted as being "better"—that is, from a higher socioeconomic class, than those who express themselves in an emotionally heated manner. My point, however, is that teammates working together can frame certain views as reflections of diversity in personality and culture and unblock potentially deadly conflicts that arise between people with seemingly irreconcilable styles who cannot comprehend one another.

There are other interesting aspects of this conflict we might consider. For example, giving the intellectual the benefit of the doubt for the moment, we could say that the essence of her message is to make life more democratic, detached, and less hurtful. Meanwhile, the essence of the activist's position is to awaken the other to her sense of superiority that reduces painful issues to mere academic discussion. The activist's point is essentially that it *is* a matter of privilege—especially for a white academic—to comment on a racist situation in a detached, "objective" way, saying essentially, "Don't be upset because you are being beaten, it is the right of the other to do that!"

Linear and Nonlinear Styles

Open Forums in diverse communities must deal with different cultural and personal styles of communication. While the forum in general uses a more linear style than ongoing, open group processes, you must make time for nonlinear, emotional interactions as well. In the beginning, invited people are asked to address the issues that are central to the forum, one after another. This sets up a linear communication style to begin with, and conveys a valuing of the mainstream approach to forums—which is, basically, one person talking after the other. It is unavoidable that, under these circumstances, some speakers take the opportunity to read prepared speeches.

After this opening format, presentations of views and dialogue about them become more spontaneous and interactive; sometimes people speak at once. Emotional interactions flair up, and you cannot always follow the interpersonal dynamics as progressing from "a to c" by way of the route "a, b, c." Sometimes you must let emotional dialogue move along its own route because core issues and feelings in everyone are involved. Moving to this deeper level holds a greater potential for clearing up feeling-related problems and creating sustainable solutions.

To help audiences prepare for the transition between the linear and nonlinear forum experiences, as a facilitator you can remind the public that spontaneous dialogue may happen, and that prepared speeches, good as they might be, are rarely tuned in to the moment.

I personally like both linear and nonlinear styles, but there are limits to everyone's capacity for following the nonlinear. Of course I, too, have my edges. I will never forget doing a large-group process in Rio de Janeiro some years ago. When the time came for the group to discuss the issues following the more formal presentations, everyone spoke at once! Dozens of voices whirled around the room, and I could not follow what was happening—and my problem was not because they were speaking in what was, for me, a foreign language. They were using English!

The reason I could not understand what was happening is because I am used to using the linear part of my mind to comprehend what people do. However, that linear mode was not useful in Rio. What amazed me even more, however, was that a few minutes later, when everything quieted down, everyone—except me—knew what had happened. Cultural differences are wonderful.

Each individual and cultural style is valuable and needed. There are linear styles as epitomized by *Robert's Rules of Order*, and there are styles that are more emotional. The following table summarizes the differences between purely linear methods that, per force, marginalize nonlinear ones, and deep democracy methods, which tend to incorporate both linear and nonlinear styles.

Linear Methods	Deep Democracy Methods
Relies on restraint and one-to-one, "a, b, c" progression	Relies on awareness of diversity, including the need for both restraint and freedom, as the moment directs
Adheres to a preconceived order or sequence, reflecting an implicit hierarchy	Awareness of a changing order going forward, backward, and diagonally
Cessation of hostility: resolution and peace viewed as the goal	Peace viewed as but one stage in an ongoing process valuing both disagreement and love

Because deep democracy is an *awareness procedure*, it is difficult to describe as a program that can be applied in a linear way. While respecting linear methods, the ordering of events is unpredictable because the facilitator, in principle, follows the nature of the moment. Here are some further points:

Listening to anger. The Open Forum facilitator needs the ability to understand the essence, or deeper message, behind what people say. For example, forum participants in an activist phase of a dialogue may pose irritating questions that cannot be answered.

For example, any answer that is given to "Why don't you know more about us?" will be wrong. The question is a kind of trap; it is not really a question at all. Rather, it is an indirect expression of agony and frustration. The resolution is to allow the agony and frustration behind the question to emerge. The basic message the activist is giving the speakers is "I dislike you because you are hurting me directly and indirectly in the following ways . . ."

Alternatively, you might say to the speakers: "Others insist that your way of speaking be more reasonable. I hear the essence of what you are telling us; we are socially shaming you and that must stop." Go for the essence of a situation that lies behind the message. Anger is important, but it is not the crucial element; people get angry if the essence is ignored.

Learning from obstreperous people. There are often folks in an Open Forum who seem to be simply obstreperous; they disagree about everything on general principles. They don't do this only at Open Forums; they do this with everyone, always. Sometimes they see themselves as bringing "the truth," or as the one individual who can stand heroically against anyone and anything, including large groups.

They confuse the situation. Sometimes they ask facilitators why they want to even hold an Open Forum. They may ask you what your goals are fifteen minutes after you stated them. Remember that in the paradigm of deep democracy, they, too, are needed. You can fight them, but I also suggest you try to enjoy them. Try to see their demeanor as a role in the group: the role of the haggler that arises when the group has not owned their doubts and pessimism.

For example, one haggler who appears regularly in Open Forums tells everyone, in the midst of it, "All this talk will never produce any-thing. You sound like a bunch of chickens squawking together." If you don't take such a statement personally, but give it back to the group, someone will eventually stand and say, "We want to try. After all, nothing else has worked until now in this community." Frequently, the community will then *really* try hard to find consensual solutions, in part, just to defeat that cantankerous voice.

Why you can't listen to some people. Have you ever heard an activist carry on in a tirade against the government? The activist will say the government is evil, bossy, bureaucratic, autocratic, patriarchal, and just downright pushy. Frequently, there is something about that activist that irritates just about everyone except for the few other activists who are clapping for her.

Understanding the many layers of such communication might help to avoid the worst for all. While the activist is speaking about an outer reality, she is unaware that her polemics—her contentious style of speaking—*is itself the ghost of the "government."* Her patriarchal behavior may be dominating or, at least, repressive. You can't blame her because the content of what she is saying cannot be debated. Since you and oth-ers listen mainly to the correct content of what she is saying, you can-not figure out why you no longer want to listen. The answer is simple. Again, the old ghost of the repressor is present in the communication style, which is completely lacking in relatedness and fellowship.

You can facilitate such moments, making transformation easier, at least momentarily, by going deeper into the activist's statements. Taking the role of the activist, you might say, "Some of us activists are talking about outer politics and the harm incurred by the uncon-sciousness of patriarchal and insensitive leadership." At another point, when resistance to the activist arises, you might say, "As activists we have been talking mainly about outer realities. Now some of us are interested in the *dreaming* government, that is the 'enemy within,' patriarchal behavior that goes unnoticed, for example, in speaking styles."

Then you might act out the behavior of that *dreaming* "govern-ment" by being pushy, then asking everyone what to do about domi-neering qualities. While speaking as this "inner enemy" you might mention you, as this figure, hope to terrify people and keep them subservient to your power! You might say that you are doing this not only because you are a power monger, but because the issues at hand are so repressed by everyone else, that you have no other choice, but to become apparently impossible in your insistence on your viewpoint.

The Psychosocial Activist and the Second Revolution

Behind your various interventions lies a new kind of psychological or political figure I call the psychosocial activist. She is interested in bringing awareness to the ghosts as well as to the issues of everyday reality. Until this point in our history, most political movements have focused mainly on government, which centrally involves the fair distribution of wealth and material goods.

These are basic entities, and their fair distribution will always be central to all Open Forums, regardless of the particular issues for which we convene. Equality and democracy involve money, food, power, and respect. Until now, revolutions have always been about the fair distribution of such things. Revolutions have been based on acts of unfairness that create pain and the terror of deprivation.

Process work is part of a new, possibly more inclusive, movement that encompasses the fair distribution of wealth and material goods, but also addresses issues of power, rank, and fellowship in communication. The reason for this new movement is simple: fair distribution of material things inhibits but does not stop the abuses of racism, sexism, and homophobia.

How does this new psychosocial activist differ from the social activist? While the social activist says, "Stop the bad guys out there," the psychosocial activist says: "Let's begin a second revolution; let's notice those bad guys in our dreaming as well. Notice how we relate to one another, right here and now." Pushy styles are always ghosts, powers used unwittingly *against people*, instead of *for relationship*.

The social activist stresses awareness of causes and effects. The social activist says, "Meditators and therapists, take a stance in the world. Make your detachment *useful*. Use your spiritual, psychological, cultural, and educational powers wisely. If you have privilege in these areas, use it in the real world, don't just keep it to yourselves."

The psychosocial activist agrees and goes further, saying: "Remember also the inner subjective dimension and the heart: otherwise your interventions are based on fear, panic, and resulting power. Use your awareness to accomplish your goals; don't get stuck in seeing only the materialism of bodies and money; otherwise you simply repeat the abuses of the past. See the spirit of the situation, and don't forget that relatedness and community are bottom lines. Notice the dreaming, the roles. Notice that history is not just a story about yesterday, but also about ghosts among us today."

Awareness work says the material things are important in this world. Fighting for them is a first revolution. The psychosocial activist is interested in a second revolution that includes the first. Notice the dreaming level as well, the fact that the spirits of greed and generosity are forces beyond the social roles of the rich or the poor, the strong or weak. Everyone must grow simultaneously in awareness. Focus on communication and dialogue. Deepen social activism.

The psychosocial activist is a hybrid of the social activist and the inner awareness worker. She knows that any message can be heard, tolerated, and respected if you notice how it is needed to make things whole.

The second revolution does not see the mainstream as the problem. There are no longer good people and bad ones. In fact, changing people's behavior is not even the goal. The goal is a combination of needed material and behavioral changes as well as awareness of the dreaming and its effects on communication and community.

The psychosocial activist manifests in her personal life what she wants to see happen politically. I think of Gandhi, who said, "Model the world you are wishing for." Today, he would say, "Model, in the moment, the world you are suggesting." If you want others to become conscious of their misuse of power, be conscious of the power you are using in the style of communication you choose to use *in this present moment.*

Revolutions are something only communities as a whole can do. Such communities constitute new social movements that do not stress the need for leaders but the need for the awareness of feelings and dreaming.

Inner Feeling as Outer Power

In the second revolution, people who do a lot of innerwork can be our guides. They notice the abuser in themselves—how they put themselves down, and how their communication style can put others down. I remember once watching a woman arguing in favor of lesbian power, suddenly switch her position to protect a homophobic man who could not understand why people of the same gender had to have relationships. He said, "I cannot understand why any of this unusual relationship stuff has to go on." Others attacked him.

She saw him freezing up, and recognized that he was being marginalized. She said that she did not want him to suffer like that. After all, she had had enough inner experience putting herself down, and did not want the same to happen to him, although the situation was reversed. She said that she did not want this person to suffer, because she already knew what that feels like from the inside. The man stuttered and almost cried.

I have always dreamed of such moments, but until then, had never seen one happen in public. The awareness, "We don't agree, and at the same time we are one another," was actually lived out and fully expressed. She used her own innerwork on her sense of oppression as a model for caring—even for her erstwhile opponent. She said, "I know what it is like inside of me to be put down and therefore I do not want you to have to feel that way." That is the psychosocial activist.

In the first revolution, we fought for awareness of position and the influence of race, sexual orientation, psychological rank, spiritual rank, etc. However, in this second revolution, I am searching for awareness of moment-to-moment experience during interactions. Consciousness of rank is the first revolution, freedom from overt oppression. The second revolution is about awareness, because freedom alone does not inhibit the oppressed—as we all know from ourselves—from re-creating another dominating environment.

Things to Remember

1. Remember to thank the elders in a community; they help your facilitation to occur.

2. Become a student. Learn from the community about its story or tale. Be a student. Value and learn from your own style. Find its eternal core.

3. Thank your team. Your team picks up whatever the whole organization is feeling. Your team can work through the same conflicts as the organization itself. So, if the Open Forum is split into opposing parts, your team will probably mirror this fragmentation as well. Teams work best when the team members accept their own diversity.

4. There is always a conflict in style between emotional and intellectual roles. Framing the situation by explaining that these are different approaches is usually helpful.

5. Activists who carry on a tirade against bossy, authoritative, and patriarchal governments may be unaware that their style *is* the "government" in the dreaming.

6. The psychosocial activist conveys, in essence, "The world is me." We need equal distribution of material possessions *and* the ongoing awareness of what is happening right now, in each moment. Valuing awareness as much as power is the second revolution.

CHAPTER 8

The Dreaming Background to Community

The second revolution is about the idea that people are part of nature, in contrast to seeing nature as part of people. The essence of nature is, to me, what the Australian Aboriginal peoples refer to as the Dreaming, a creative energy that gives rise to everything. In other words, what people refer to as *reality* is not a fact, but an idea arrived at through social conditioning.

There are as many realities as there are cultures and periods of history. The present cosmopolitan reality is based on time, space, and material things. Another reality is the Dreaming, the world of deep feelings and vague fantasies that we sense preceding concrete decision making.

The Dreaming is to everyday reality as the quantum world is to the Newtonian reality. The Dreaming shakes our certainty that life is composed of real people in fixed bodies. To truly understand, appreciate, and even love the community you are working for, you need to sense it not only as a fact composed of real people, but as a Dreaming essence that evolves into the changing roles, timespirits, and people. Timespirits are cultural, collective figures such as the "abuser," the "heroine," etc., which are changing spirits of the times.

In a certain sense, the Dreaming and its timespirits are more fundamental than everyday reality, because timespirits precede roles and even linger on after we have filled these roles and died! In this chapter, I want to apply the concepts of the Dreaming to understand and work with various kinds of people-problems such as hopelessness, leaving communities, attacking authorities, and longing for freedom.

Hopelessness

In many Open Forums, at one point or another, someone inevitably stands up and says, "What can I do? I am only one little person in this big world; I can do nothing." This feeling of hopelessness is a widespread problem around the world that seems to make people give up on trying to solve problems in their own families, let alone organizations, cities, nations, and the planet.

There are many reasons for statements of hopelessness. To begin with, the person who made the statement is cut off from her own sense of the Dreaming that creates, re-creates, destroys, and rearranges everything. Therapists try to work on such problems on a one-to-one basis, but these problems seem to me to belong to whole communities and cultures as well.

Hopelessness is due to whole cultures marginalizing fantasy and creativity, art and music—in brief, the mysteriousness of everyday life. Because I travel a great deal, I know that certain cultures do not marginalize the Dreaming. Australian Aboriginal people, indigenous African shamans, first-nation people in the Americas, etc., still take the Dreaming seriously, each in their own way.

In other words, one reason for hopelessness is cultural attitudes that marginalize the Dreaming. In a way, the first racist act is to look down on the Dreaming, on people and cultures that are interested in the Dreamtimes. One momentary way of dealing with this in Open Forum settings is to ask people about their dreams, about songs that suddenly come to their minds, about their ability to dance and create theater from forum issues after the forum has ended. There are as many ways to bring the Dreaming back as there are humans on this Earth.

A second reason that someone in a forum complains of hopelessness is because she may be unable to protect herself from the forum as a whole. If you use your facilitator's awareness to notice edges, you may have noticed that someone else oppressed her in a way she may not have consciously noticed. If no one noticed, she not only feels injured, but also incapable of sharing the problem with others. Solution? Go back to the preceding statements and see how they may have put that person down.

Negative historical generalizations about what's wrong with the world, or insinuations that nothing can be changed or that events are over-powering or distant from where we are now, make people feel hopeless. Derisive statements about the governments "out there" or about power-ful multinational organizations "out there" are themselves oppressive.

Comments such as, "Those in control have so much power and money that we few individuals are powerless against them" are oppres-sive statements because they imply that we are powerless; nothing can be done. This is where awareness work comes front and center by point-ing out that the self-proclaimed victim's behavior is, in essence, filled with ghosts. In this case, the governments or multinationals are ghosts.

The depressed individual is speaking of the Dreaming, the deep background to the forum, the covert level in which the persecutor has become a ghost. The "multinational" that ignores local, small, "insignificant," moment-to-moment feelings is present in the forum right now, in this very room and place, in each and every person. Therefore, you can respond to such voices in several ways.

You can say, for example, that those multinationals are big and tough and distant, but they are also here in this room. Then get up and play that multinational, and tell everyone that they are insignificant, and that they should forget whatever personal feelings they may have. You can say that governments and multinationals are "real," but that they are also roles created by the Dreaming that neglects Itself!

On the other hand, you can forget terms such as "the Dreaming" and say, "Let's look at the power we have here today and see how to use it best!" For example, consider the nonlocal influence of the Open Forum. Groups working on raising their level of consciousness influ-ence the world around them in unforeseen ways. You can track how Open Forum interactions affect public and mainstream opinion long after the end of the forum.

The Deep Democracy of Open Forums

I recently corresponded with a newspaper in a town where we had conducted an Open Forum about racism. The newspaper people told me that since the forum, the city media have awakened to the forum's topic. There are all sorts of discussions about racism, and the students in the schools and universities are upset about racism and even did a sit-in at the university around racial harassment. This is the first time that has happened since the 1960s. Large companies in that area, interviewed by the media, reported having more awareness about racial issues. Even in the most conservative part of that city, there were reports of people complaining in the schools about racial harassment! Forums have "ripple" effects that contribute to change, even if all change is temporary.

Remember that, historically, the Open Forum was created, in part, as a reaction to the distance between those in power and the individual citizens. Open Forums arose, in part, to give individuals the sense of having an impact on their governments. In an Open Forum, what you say *as an individual* has power. The forum is a reaction to the distant multinational and governmental powers that (may inadvertently) depotentiate citizens.

Furthermore, history is testimony to great movements of individuals and groups that changed history. I think of U.S. civil rights groups and groups in the sixties that stopped the Vietnam War. I recall the Velvet Revolution in Czechoslovakia, the Solidarity Movement in Poland, and the "People Power Movement" in the Philippines.

Every time we ignore the Dreaming—the feelings we have, and the differences between our ideas and those of others—we avoid diversity issues and, symbolically speaking, become a "multinational." At a recent forum we facilitated between the roles of the World Trade Organization and the International Monetary Fund, on the one side, and trade unions and individual protestors, on the other, the WTO and IMF were called "global crooks who neglect the local situation in countries." There were *huge* revelations to everyone present on both sides:

Every time we favor orderly meetings over heated exchanges, we not only conflict with conflict, but end up repressing the "local" experiences.

Every time we favor a one-at-a-time style over dialogue and process, we forward separation.

Most people would favor "local" experiences and "dialogue and process" but are afraid to do so because they don't know how to deal with heated exchanges.

I remember one amazing exchange that occurred when a man, speaking for the WTO, said that the protestors were "young flakes who knew nothing of the world." The protestor being attacked told him in a face-to-face interaction, "You remind me of my father, who is not the least bit interested in anyone or anything but his theories of the world." For some unexplained reason, that man's eyes looked so sad, hearing himself described as uninterested in anything but himself, that the "protestor" touched his hand in a gesture of compassion, and they both wept, then embraced each other.

They left the world economic "realities" and entered the Dreaming. Both were changed radically by what occurred. My point is not that this particular exchange between these two men changed the world in one moment, or that the men themselves were permanently altered for the better, but that global issues ignore individual situations and that if we are not personal, then we are all multinationals. To create a more fluid process worldwide, moving between global issues and individual situations, we need awareness.

We get fed up with the state of the world mainly because of one problem: the Dreaming aspect of our lives—personal awareness and interactions, inside of us and outside—is marginalized. Help organizations wake up to their ghosts, and help yourself wake up to the global ghost in you.

The Abuser as Fact and Ghost

Finding the evil on the outside is so supported by our everyday reality that we forget that evil is also a ghost, part of the Dreaming. Take the case of X, who hurts people, dominates them, pushes them around, and finally gets caught and accused of all that. Most folks are happy when this occurs, but I am always a bit sad. I know that everyone who knew X before all the abuse occurred is also responsible for what happened. Everyone who has witnessed X's tiny transgressions over the years and said nothing, everyone who has witnessed things going wrong and said nothing is responsible.

We readily recognize the abuser "in the flesh," while ignoring the ghost of the abuser that we project onto the abuser. He or she could only have done harmful things because the ghost of the abuser in the rest of us allowed those things to happen. The abuser *was* (and still may be) insensitive, that's true! But we, in the ghost role of the abuser, were and may still be insensitive to what we saw as well.

Thus, if you are guilty, then I as a witness am guilty of insensitivity as well. In Dreaming, there is no such thing as a purely local problem that is not also global, and of course, no global problem that is not instantaneously local.

With awareness of Dreaming, each of us must say:

"I am the person from a disenfranchised group in this country, suffering, and angry at the mainstream for abusing those of us who could not defend ourselves."

"I am the mainstream person hated because of history, and because I ignore any issues that are not mine today."

"I am the one who cannot defend herself against public abuse in a racist world except by turning violent."

"I am the gay person rejected by her own family, and I am the family rejecting gays."

"I am the person in a multiracial or multicultural relationship who is disliked by all races for what they call my 'audacity.'"

"I am different from others, and the one who ignores my special nature."

"I am the future, praying for understanding and compassion that includes everyone."

"I am the Open Forum participant looking for a facilitator who will protect me against herself, myself, and others."

Preaching to the Choir

In many Open Forums, someone who wants to deflate the power of the group will stand up and say something like, "You are just preaching to the choir, to those already converted."

How do you deal with that? What is the Dreaming underneath the comment? One possibility is that the individual speaking the complaint is playing the role of the hero, some lone individual who takes a stand against everyone. So you might say to that individual, "I am on your side; let's take a stand not just against everyone in this room, but against everyone, everywhere. What is our basic point?" If the hero is really the role emerging at this moment from the Dreaming, the individual will now speak about something that has been insufficiently addressed.

You might also see the choir as a role that has not been identified yet and admit, "Yes, it's true, everybody in the room is, in one way or another, interested in a given topic, otherwise we would not be here. After all, we are here either because we have to attend because we are part of the organization, or because we are interested in the theme for a number of reasons." A given group may be composed of folks from mainly lower economic classes, or from the middle class or upper class. Some groups will be mainly one race or nationality. Some groups have a majority of social activists present.

However, this is where the answer to the statement about being a choir changes from "Yes, it's true," to a "No, you are wrong." You can say to the person accusing the community of being no more than a choir:

> "No, a given group is a choir in the sense that it is seemingly homogenous, but that is only because it is repressing its own conflicts in the moment. The problems in each group are the same: hurt and anger. The ones on top are afraid of those below and therefore marginalize them. Revolt is always imminent whenever members of the human race come together!"

> "No, if we only were like a choir, you could relax for a few minutes. That is really not the case here. Very few people are relaxed, and even fewer are thinking about singing praises to God—or to anyone."

> "No, as far as the world as a whole is concerned, there are rarely any choirs—even in those "good" groups trying to help the world, such as religious groups. In fact, even the Process Work Center of Portland is anything but a choir! All groups, regardless of how wonderful their visions may be, are a small hologram of the world. Hospitals, the UN, the Red Cross are just pieces of the world itself, since they are full of the same conflicts."

People Leaving the Forum

Some forum facilitators feel threatened or insulted if a few of the participants leave early. "Do Not Go" is the nonverbal message. As all eyes track one person going to the door, some think, "That person left; that must be significant." Now let us consider why people leave.

Some real people with real bodies have to go to the bathroom!

Some have no more time to spare. Keep the meetings down to two hours (an hour and a half is a little short). People are busy with their everyday lives; just showing up means they are trying to do *something*.

Some get antsy or are bored. Perhaps you missed the hot spots, and therefore the group is cycling around and not getting to the emotional point. Or perhaps that person has a short attention span, no matter how compelling the stimulus.

Remember that the person who leaves is still there in the Dreaming in the form of a ghost role. The *person* and the *role* are not the same. Even if someone leaves, the role remains. Perhaps nature, the Tao, wants that role to be shared by everyone in the room and not pinned on only the person who has left. If someone is no longer there, accept the group the way it is.

Ask the participants what they imagine being the reason for the person's departure. If they think the person left out of fear, then fear is a ghost.

Some who leave early are expressing their disagreement by walking out. Marginalized groups in the 1960s often left forum-type gatherings as a way to protest the mainstream.

Marginalized groups may want to gather without the so-called oppressor being present. Let them. Remember: *people leave, but roles stay!* If those who are marginalized leave, then the ghost of marginalization in the remaining participants can become more conscious, and everyone can see just what was projected onto the "victims."

If a person in the midst of a fight marches out, she may have reached her "edge"—the limit of what she feels she can say or do. Perhaps she became angry and wanted to leave to cool off. Take her place; speak as if you were she. Go over her edge (for her, so to speak) and try to speak the inexpressible, imagining into her role.

In large forums, having a teammate at the door may be very comforting for people arriving and departing. When folks enter, they are greeted as individuals. In addition, when they leave—no matter when—they are respectfully bade good-bye.

The Rank of Speaking Out

Have you been at meetings where a few powerful people speak, and the others remain quiet? Many people do not speak because they do not have enough personal power to do so. Power and rank are relative concepts, depending on a given issue and situation. For example, in a discussion about economics, racism, or sexism, a person of color or a woman may feel more justified in speaking up at certain moments than a white man. In a discussion about men's issues, a man might feel like he has the rank to speak up. In a basically mainstream group, someone from a marginalized community will be afraid to speak. Rank is cumulative and multidimensional, and even if the issue is "yours," you may remain quiet.

In one of my group process classes in Portland, I experimented with rank to find out more about why some people speak out in public while others do not. To explore this area, I asked people to give their various social attributes a number, ranking each with a one, two, or three, depending on whether they felt that the attribute had low, medium, or high rank within the community. We played with numbers, not taking them very seriously, to get a feel for the situation. The question I posed was "In relation to your community, what do you feel your rank is in the areas of gender, race, sexual orientation, age, health, spiritual connectedness, economics, education, social status in the given community, psychological well-being, and linguistic ability?" I did not define these attributes but let the people do so for themselves.

We found that whether someone spoke out in public during a discussion depended not on the rank of any single attribute, but on his or her cumulative rank. Given the eleven categories and the three scores in each category (one, two, or three for low, medium, and high, respectively), the maximum possible score was thirty-three, the minimum was eleven, and the median score for cumulative rank was twenty-two. Imagine that you are from a given organization and attending an

Open Forum, and rank yourself using the list below. How many points do you have? (You may want to add other categories to this list.)

Social Topic	Rank or Power: 1, 2, or 3
Race	
Gender	
Sexual orientation	
Age	
Spiritual connectedness	
Health	
Economic	
Education	
Social rank in given group	
Psychological well-being	
Linguistic ability	
Your total sum = (22 is "average")	

I completed the chart above for myself, imagining I was in an Open Forum in a large business organization in the U.S. Being a healthy, educated, white, heterosexual man, etc., gave me a lot of rank. But relative to that group, I was low in social rank, and as a result, low in psychological well-being, also. My overall score was median, which is why I was a bit nervous working for that business. This score gave me the impulse to do more innerwork to know the higher-ranking people as figures in myself.

My Portland class found that if you had a cumulative rank of less than nineteen, you would not speak up! I would bet that if you have a score of less than twenty-one, it is hard for you to speak up in a given situation. If you scored above twenty-one, you probably feel confident in your group. In another group or context, you will have more or less rank, depending on the moment and the situation.

Thus, rank is cumulative and relative to a particular group and theme. The bottom line is that facilitators need to be sensitive to and aware of the effects of rank and power on themselves and the participants. Rank and power are ghosts; they never show themselves directly. However, you can surely feel them in your body! In what groups and on what themes will you be able to speak, or not speak?

In groups where many people are quiet, you may want to create another Open Forum to follow that process, such as a forum done on paper or via e-mail. One of the advantages of e-mail is that people can create pseudonyms and consequently feel freer to speak out than in public. When people do not have to sign their own names next to a comment, it is quite amazing what they have to say. Working through e-mail is a huge and fascinating topic by itself, which I will take up later.

My Own Awareness Learning

Because I suggest that facilitators share what they have learned with their teams and the public, perhaps I may be allowed to do so here. I would like to discuss what I recently learned by studying a videotape of an Open Forum where the mayor of the city was one of the invited speakers. I suspect my learning might apply to other facilitators as well. Here is what happened.

To introduce himself and his viewpoint at a forum on racism, the mayor spoke for five minutes. In this forum, he clearly wanted to demonstrate that he is not racist by telling a story from his childhood. In this story about a mostly white, small town in the Midwest, the mayor described his openhearted attitude toward the one African American kid in town. He said the child felt rejected because of racist signs on one of the town's store windows. The child got angry and committed some petty crime, for which he was placed in juvenile hall. Finally, the boy was let out of confinement and returned to school, where he helped the school team win a ball game.

After the mayor spoke, showing how "nonracist" he was by liking that boy, I could not refrain from pointing something out to him about racism. I said, in my most serious tone, that by focusing on that child as the one committing a petty crime, he was buying into the stereotypical image of a troublesome kid of a certain race, an image forwarded by the media. His image is racist insofar as neither the child nor the African American community can easily protect themselves against these stereotypes. I was very upset.

While watching myself on film, I was shocked to see how I dealt with that mayor. I acted politely, but it was clear that I was hiding my real feelings. The content of my words pointed out how the mayor was inadvertently racist in his remarks, but I noticed that in my behavior, I was not just upset about what he was doing to others; I secretly felt superior to him. Then I remembered the feeling I had when I had spoken to the mayor. I had thought, "He's the mayor of the city and I feel better and more insightful than he." I was happy that I had pointed out hurtful behavior. However, I was upset with myself because I had treated him as if he were an icon, not a human being, and because I secretly felt superior. I was happy to notice that the mayor apparently did not seem to notice *my* behavior!

In my defense you might think, "Come on, that's not so serious, and besides, the interaction must have gone well, the outcome was good." However, I am not happy with myself. The content of what I said was fine: "Don't put down people by inadvertently stereotyping them." However, my behavior had another message: "I am putting you down because you are the stereotypical unconscious mayor." In other words, by focusing on the reality of the situation, I did not notice the Dreaming, and hence fell into being the very ghost I was attacking!

If I had been aware of myself, I might still have said what I did about stereotyping *and*, at the same time, said, "I am here as one of the facilitators, but I notice the educator and social activist in me turning against you, dear mayor. The educator wants to suggest new information, and the social activist wants to right a wrong. However, I notice that I lost track of you as a human being. I am a stereotyper as well, ignoring you as a human being in the role of the mayor!"

You might think I am carrying all this too far, but awareness is my goal, not just social action. As long as I am only a righteous activist in momentary denial of his own sense of superiority, I am merely replacing old hierarchies with new ones, with righteous educators who believe *they* are superior.

I feel sad about my unconsciousness, even though the mayor did not seem to notice anything. I lost track that both he and I were human beings in roles. At such times, when my teammates or I notice these things about me, the content of my social action always goes over better, in part because the entire Dreaming is taken into consideration. During such times, the forum is more like a sailboat carried by the wind, instead of a rowboat propelled with effort by oars.

Hot Spots and Chaos

A hot spot occurred during the heated Open Forum I just mentioned with the mayor. I especially want to thank Gary Reiss for having created that forum; he was unusually courageous in all that happened there. After the mayor spoke in the beginning of the forum, an invited neo-Nazi Ku Klux Klan member took the floor. (Those in the KKK calling themselves "neo-Nazis" dislike Jews, Blacks, Asians, gays, or anyone who is not Aryan and heterosexual.) He said, unabashedly: "Our group does not think it is right that different groups live together. Groups should be segregated." As he spoke, a liberal activist raised his voice to the volume and pitch of the KKK man and began speaking simultaneously. Blasting forth to drown out the KKK viewpoint, the liberal raged and spoke so that no one could understand the Klansman. The liberal said, "No one should have to listen to that junk. It is anti-American, old-fashioned, and antidemocratic!"

It seemed as if the hundreds of people at that forum began speaking simultaneously. *Everyone* started talking at once as both men spoke over each other. The two viewpoints, the KKK and the liberal, were symmetrical in only one respect: both contended that the other should *not* be listened to.

The noise level rose in the room, and chaos was rife. But the sense of chaos is usually a statement about consensus reality only. In the Dreaming, there is a clear pattern. My awareness statement was simply: "It's okay if two people speak simultaneously. I know that it is difficult for some when two polarized positions are being voiced at the same time. In mainstream cultures in the United States, speaking at the same time is frowned on, but the cultural viewpoint that assumes that only one person should speak at a time is just one viewpoint. Let them speak simultaneously. Trust them, give them a chance." Their heated interaction abated in a couple of minutes and the forum proceeded, allowing many people to speak and be heard.

A few people were upset that a racist was allowed to speak, while others supported the dialogue, claiming that this very kind of *open* polarization was the essence of democracy.

I learned a lot. That liberal felt insulted by our having invited someone from the KKK, although the invited speakers had been announced early in the forum's advertisement. I should have expected that conflict to arise. I had forgotten how shocking it is to hear someone speak from a marginal position in a public forum.

Moreover, I should have sensed, knowing myself, that activists rarely work well with one another, each feeling her or his liberal position "is the best and only." I could have said: "Your position is important; you are an elder in this city. Thank you for your work." Then I might have also added: "My position is different. I want to listen to the most disturbing voices here, so that they feel heard and are not forced to resort to guns elsewhere." Open Forums may reduce violence in the workplace and in the city, *but only if all voices are heard.*

Are You a Person or a Spirit?

Though the above figures are clearly roles, most people do not fit neatly into one role or another, but are really a mixture of races, sexual orientations, religions, and health issues, and may have both lower and higher ranked positions (within any given organization). Who is *only* "the boss," the "disturber," the "brain," "the Nazi?"

Nevertheless, it is not easy to get out of a role when others always identify you as being in that one and only role. For example, when you are in a minority role within a given social or organizational context— when you are in the one-down position, at one time or another—you may experience the impulse to "hide" yourself by identifying with the mainstream so that you will not be hurt by those above.

Others in your group become irritated with you because they experience your tendency to hide as a desertion. If you are a successful woman but do not "stand for" women, your female colleagues may think you are a deserter. A Jew, Hispanic, gay, or Black who does not defend or praise being Jewish, Hispanic, gay or Black will be criticized by his or her group as being internally anti-Semitic, internally homophobic, or racist, etc.

Recall the interaction I mentioned earlier (in chapter 3) between a Black Panther and a woman who identified herself as a mixture of Irish and African American. We were at a very tense moment in that Open Forum in Houston, organized around the murder of James Byrd, an African American who had been brutally slain in Jasper, Texas. A conflict suddenly erupted between the Panthers and others in the African American community over the issue of identifying with being black and dropping any other racial admixtures. The woman exclaimed, "My mother is Irish and my father African, so I am not one thing or another." The Panther said, "Sister, you were born black, you've grown up black, and you are going to die black!"[1]

I have heard a similar conversation in every minority community. Which side of the conversation is right or correct? Both. Every one of us is born into consensus reality—this physical world—with certain genes, and we are therefore seen as being Black, African, African American, Hispanic, Italian, Irish, Jewish, Native American, Japanese, Korean, Chinese, and so on. We are born with or acquire certain health issues, sexual orientations, etc.

The message of that Black Panther was that we cannot marginalize the social reality of cultural prejudice. You cannot avoid your appearance, for more than a few minutes; you cannot avoid your sexual orientation or your religious beliefs for long. At the same time, the woman was telling us, "Don't marginalize the realm of the individual." As far as cultural reality is concerned, we may be identified with a particular racial role; yet, *at the same time*, as spiritual beings, we are free, liberated from any form at all. We are like everything else in this universe— stardust, pieces of the infinite.

It seems to me that we can't congruently stand for our social role if we do not appreciate spiritual freedom. In addition, we cannot feel spiritually free if we have not identified completely with our position as a human being within the confining social contexts of this planet. Reality and Dreaming are inseparable.

Things to Remember

1. Expressions of hopelessness can be due to reaching an edge, a reaction against having been publicly downed and unable to protect oneself. Hopelessness may also be due to the impossibility of dealing with generalities about history and power-holders not represented in the moment. Represent these entities as ghost roles. Remember that the notion of multinational corporations can be a projection of our own tendency to ignore individuals by "globalizing" or "generalizing." The Open Forum is a reaction to all forms of hopelessness about social change.

2. There is no choir to preach to; in fact, the forum—and every group—is a conglomeration similar to the world itself.

3. People leave the forum early for a variety of reasons. Yet they have not left entirely, for the role that they "brought" to the forum in the apparent form of their personhood exists independent of them in the form of a ghost role that will always be present wherever there are humans. Therefore, let folks come and go as they like.

4. It is common to criticize or denigrate authorities, but remember that the critic who is doing the downing may be an "authority" as well. To change the world, do as much inner as outer changing.

5. Chaos and escalation around hot spots are scary, but if you suggest trusting the people in the heat to do their best, if you focus and listen, escalation becomes less necessary.

6. We are our social roles, and we are free of all roles. Like everything else in this universe, we are a mixture of stardust, a piece of the infinite, and can therefore be proud of our particular mixture. Reality and Dreaming are inseparable.

CHAPTER 9

The Media as a Wake-up Dream

Open Forums held in organizations and cities create a lot of "buzz"—that is, gossip and public interest. After all, the forum is dealing with questions that have been underground or, at least, only a matter of gossip until now. Since one of the goals of the forum is to attract attention and to raise people's awareness of the issues at hand, it is not surprising when this new awareness creates even more "buzz." Large Open Forums attract public media attention, such as newspapers, radio, TV, Internet, and other public broadcasting mechanisms. Therefore, I see working with the media as part of your work as a facilitator of an Open Forum. The media is another way in which the Dreaming behind the forum expresses itself.

There are various levels to this buzz, two of which are the inner buzz in your head (your own inner applause, criticism, and dreams about the forum) and the level of buzz coming from the outer media with whom you must now deal as the forum ends.

Composition of the Media

Before pondering how to relate to the media, let us consider what or who they are. I think of the media as a huge radio antenna sending out signals to the surrounding world. In the sketch, the Open Forum is linked to the media in the center of the picture. The media relates to everyone outside the forum, to the people distributed throughout the organization's or the city's "field."

How the Media Communicates with the Rest of the World (Organization or City)

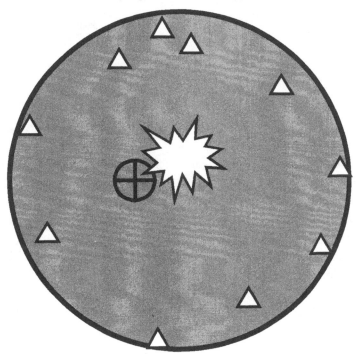

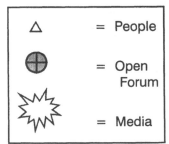

△	= People
⊕	= Open Forum
✺	= Media

The media connects to the periphery in a manner we cannot easily do by ourselves as individuals. Of course, we are all part of the media, especially with our so-called "bush" telephone—our personal interconnections, our one-to-one contacts. The bush telephone is still a major way of advertising. Therefore, the media concept includes the bush telephone, the newspaper, TV, radio, internet, books, movies, art projects, and theater.

The media operates in the world as a big dream operates inside an individual. The media is to the world as a big dream is to a sleeping person. The media seems to see its audience as a bunch of sleeping people needing a wake-up call. It feels it must catch our attention by blasting in our ears with astounding and shocking news.

Little dreams may not wake you up, but big dreams will. Tom Atlee, in his website, stresses that the media can also be a little dream, in the negative sense. A little dream is the kind that keeps you hypnotized and sleeping! For example, "Buy the paper, only fifty cents" is a hypnotic induction telling you this is a bargain—when it may not be. A big dream makes you ponder, "What has happened?" Little dreams let you forget and go back to sleep. Some mornings you wake up with a big dream still in awareness: God appeared. Your friends were killed in a big fire. You were chased by beings from another planet.

Media Dualism

The popular media is dualistic in the sense that there are always two or more apparently irreconcilable and irreducible viewpoints presented, and rarely any interaction between them. Usually one is good and the other evil. In short, there is no process between these two supposedly fixed states of the system. Most media bring only minimal understanding of either side; it seems that either understanding is rare or it does not sell well. Among themselves, newscasters say "nothing's happening," when there are no disasters. No splash. Most publishers I know are similar: "Splash books sell." The alternative or underground media are not much different in the sense of presenting the sides as irreducibly good and evil. Few seem interested in genuine dialogue between opposing sides.

The media sees life in polarized terms of success or failure. There are few nuances or gradations. It is either this country *or* that one; it is all about the rich *or* the poor, liberals *or* conservatives, the guilty *or* the innocent. It is important to understand the media because they are "dreamed up" from within each of us. By "dreamed up," I mean that dreamlike events inside of us may not be directly represented, but "dream themselves up" on the outside, so to speak. Dreaming up implies that the dream world seeks to realize itself in everyday life!

Dualism is the basic philosophy most of us employ when we engage in self-criticism. You are good, or you are bad—and usually you are bad. You either succeed at something or you fail. You are smart, or you are stupid. You are good-looking or ugly.

Sound Bites

Media interviews are inevitably conducted in this oppositional style. Imagine, for example, that the Open Forum you have been working in is now ending. Someone from the press shoves a microphone in front of your face and asks you questions. What is happening? If you use your awareness, and go slowly, you will notice that the interviewer is treating you as if your viewpoint is important enough to hear. But is your viewpoint more important than others? Why not ask the interviewer why are you being interviewed and who will be ignored, in order to know which ghosts to include in your comments?

Often the interview is adversarial in nature. The news may try to polarize your view so that it is good or evil, so that another interviewee at another point, confronted with the same questions, will take the opposite stance. The media is usually not as interested in the gradations, or various roles within you, that is the full story, as it is in the battle between opposing positions. Like a boxing match, you are in one corner, and an opponent is waiting in the other corner. Each round must be brief and to the point; after all, this must be *entertaining*. This is how the media participates in forwarding conflict and war.

During the recent war in Kosovo, I remember a newspaper person asking me, "How do we solve the war in Kosovo? Please answer in one minute." Where should I have begun? I said, "Well, you have to start at the beginning of the universe. Ten billion years ago."

Alternatively, I could start with the essence of that question, which is really aimed at a public that will only read for one minute. I said, "The origin of war is your type of question, in wanting simple solutions to complex and longstanding animosities instead of insights into how to work on relationship problems. The origin of war is *anywhere* and *everywhere*. The origin of war is due not only to the warring participants, but to the public viewpoint that only wants one-sided solutions and is not willing to tolerate or explore the entire complexity of an issue. The war out there is a picture of how we deal with our own relationships."

Self-Importance versus Awareness

If you get to the point where you are being interviewed and the media treats you as if you are important enough to be heard, at first you may become shy or bigheaded. The symptom of either condition is getting nervous, which is a response to being encouraged to leave your own inner way and now play a one-sided public role.

If you are awake, you can remember that *the only real power that you yourself can own is awareness.* Awareness tells you that socially wielded power is tied up with the spirits of the times, with particular roles, one of which you are now being asked to play. From the media's viewpoint you may be important as a role, but from another viewpoint, you are not a role; you are a person, with many roles inside of you.

If you are psychosocial activist, you might say that the role you choose to play is one that forwards everyone's awareness that each of us is responsible for filling roles. You can say that the role of the facilitator is to get various sides to listen to and get to know one another. And you might explain that the forum process did not stop with the end of the forum, but is continuing everywhere at the moment. Under these circumstances you can tell the media they may take the role of one side or the other side. However, your basic role is that of an *awareness* coach.

When the media asks if you are satisfied with what happened at the forum, you might as well state your personal opinion, remembering any gains in awareness that may have occurred. However, your awareness tells you that, even while you are being interviewed, various ghost roles are also present.

The Deep Democracy of Open Forums

There is the role you are playing; there is the media as a role, and the role of a reader who will be critical of what you are saying. Therefore, feel your way into the role of someone who will disagree with your evaluation of the Open Forum and say, "We should see the forum from another viewpoint, which does not care about awareness but is interested only in results. Both viewpoints are valuable, etc."

Some facilitators avoid the media because it is so polarizing. However, dealing with the media can be just another form of awareness work. Then you know that the media is like your inner critic who says, in a very one-sided manner, "You are responsible for all the things, the good and the bad, and especially for what went 'wrong' at the forum." Yet, awareness also tells you there is another viewpoint that says, "I didn't do anything, the community does things together. People and nature and the community do things together. The Dreaming is behind everything, not people."

Taking Events out of Context

The media is likely to take the forum and your work out of the context of the social, educational, financial, and organizational issues at hand and make up another, entirely different, story about what is happening. The media is not an objective observer, reporting the news the way it is. It is a storyteller and relates to group myths of the day. In the example of the KKK that I discussed in chapter 8, the question of racism was not half as important to the media as the story that flashed across the headlines of a city paper the next morning: "Mindells Invite the KKK to an Open Forum!"

Those newspaper headlines went so far that even my aunt, from the opposite part of the country, heard about the event and approached me at the beginning of the next family gathering, a year and a half after the event. She cornered Amy and me and exclaimed to me, "How dare you, inviting those Nazis to speak! How can you call yourself a Jew!" She had a point. I weakly defended myself, trying to explain that actually I do not refer to myself as a Jew first, but as a person.

However, my argument went over with her like a load of bricks falling into water. She was not the least bit interested in anything but the roles of the Jew and the Nazi. That is exactly what the media hoped for—the polarization between the democratic public and the Nazi bigot!

Nevertheless, that family event turned out to be one of the best for me. I had to see her point. How can a Jew invite a Nazi to air her or his views? On the other hand, my counterpoint was, yes, I am a Jew, and no, I am not only a Jew. Although I love my genes and my ethnic background, at times, I am not only those genes. Besides, the focus of the forum was not the KKK but a reduction in the racism in the city reported on by that newspaper. My aunt actually agreed and saw my point.

In any case, the media story—like my good aunt—focused on the KKK and not the more significant topic of racism. As the forum was closing, the media's first question was, "How did you dare invite that neo-Nazi?" The media took the forum out of the context of the larger issue, namely, getting to the roots of racism. The moral of the story is to encourage the media to *remember the context*.

I should have said to them: "Your question about the KKK is out of context; it is about another story, which catches the public's attention but is not the core issue here. Please record what I tell you. Consider the larger picture. As a reporter, you must care for the whole truth about the roots of racism. I understand that neo-Nazis make splash money for the papers, whereas dealing with the roots of racism is subtle, and may not be income producing."

By the way, your inner critic usually works the same way as the media. The inner critic always takes what you have done out of context. He, she, or "it" uses the same psychology. "Forget the context and the larger goal you are involved in reaching. Forget history, and forget everyone. Forget your dream for humanity. You are either good or bad, and this time you are bad!" The critic's comments are out of context. Inside or out, add the viewpoint that stresses awareness of the context, history, and larger goals.

Subtle, Splashless Events

The mainstream mind is interested in crash and splash and in simplicity, but real events do not fit into the categorizations of either simple or complex. A process-oriented view is that we are interested not only in crash and splash, but also in dialogue between the parts. Dealing with trauma and history takes time and requires dialogue between parts that change slowly.

Dialogue does not make money; it is beyond complex and simple and requires subtle awareness of changes in feeling. We cannot measure the results of such dialogue; it meanders in a more circuitous, nonlinear manner. All this takes patience. The purpose of the forum is not to solve the world's problems, but to reawaken participants to their diversity—both as individuals and as a large group—so that the process of community can begin.

Using the Splash

Until now, I myself have been like the media in portraying it as being "bad." Yet, the media is neither good nor bad. It is simply part of the overall Open Forum process. In fact, as a facilitator, you can get into their role and use "their" splash process as if it were your own. After all, since most alternative and mainstream media use people to create good and evil stories, why not *use* the media instead of being used by them? If you are a passive victim relative to the media, you are bound to see it as "evil" while you remain the "good" person, its "victim." However, when you are aware of the dreaming process involved, you can enter the role of the media, and use oppositional and "splash thinking" to create your own story.

You might say to yourself: "I realize that I too can be dualistic at times. Now I would like to create the story." Remember that the mainstream part of everyone's mind tends to sleep. Use the "Wake Up! Buy Me!" splash to create more awareness in yourself. To do that, write out your own media story before the forum begins. Describe what is trying to happen in your inner organization or city. Create the story that is driving you. It is the story *you* want to make conscious to all. Moreover, that story is the power dreaming you up to be a facilitator.

For example, in the story I might write about that particular forum, there would be less abuse of, and greater respect for, all people in that city. In the Open Forum I have been speaking about, my story is as follows:

Arnold Mindell, Ph.D.

Once upon a time there was a city where most people went to sleep so early they did not notice that, at night, some folks stayed up to hurt others. Those who were hurt could not stand it anymore, and those creating the hurt did not want to think about it. Moreover, everyone else continued to sleep. One day some weird folks came to town and made a big fire to attract the interest of a bunch of people who stayed up late enough to see the fire in the center of town. It was a small fire, but bright enough to attract people to come and look. Then, once some of the sleepy townspeople gathered around the fire, they began to wake up and heard all sorts of stories.

For the first time they heard people who were hurt talk to people who had created the hurt. Everyone considered what to do about the situation and discovered that racism requires consciousness of human interactions at every moment of the day and night. They realized that racism is a deep problem, but is still only the tip of an iceberg containing all the other "-isms" in the world.

The insights about racism made the fire sparkle. Some people lit or rather relit their own candles from the great fire, and carried the candles home.

Many years have now passed since that first fire. The amazing thing is that even though many people died and many were born, the fire still remains in the center of town. It is the most amazing fire. If it is not tended to, it sometimes threatens to burn down the town. Otherwise, it is a constant source of heat and light, even on the coldest nights. The people renamed their city after that fire, calling their town "Sitting Round the Fire," which is one of my stories.

Looking back at the results of the forum, aspects of the story came true. The front pages of the morning papers carried the splash about the KKK member. National Public Radio, the TV, and other media got interested. There was a lot of attention given to the issue; the fire kindled others, and more people got involved, creating more forums, and awareness improved a bit in that city.

The point is that a splash can be used for the benefit of all. The media is the splash-maker in all that we do. We can all use the splash by making our own stories when interviewed on the topics at the end of the forum.

141

The Deep Democracy of Open Forums

The Significance of the Interviewer

No story is absolute and unchanging. No story is "objective," but always includes the interviewers. So bring them in. This is what happened during the interviews following the forum in that city:

> *Interviewer from the leading paper: Dr. Mindell, why did you invite a neo-Nazi and what is your educational background and your experience in this area?*
>
> *Amy: You look like a mainstream person; please tell me what your ethnicity is.*
>
> *Interviewer: Why do you ask something like that?*
>
> *Amy: You just asked me similar questions, and I would like to know with whom I am speaking. Please be kind enough to tell me where you come from and who you are. The public needs to know as much about you as what happened here this evening. After all, we are both roles in the field.*

That interviewer turned off her tape recorder and proceeded to tell me a touching story about herself. She told me that she was extremely interested in diversity issues because of her own sexual orientation. I thanked her and said that inviting a neo-Nazi was like inviting someone who was overtly homophobic. I explained that *not* listening to one-sided hate groups only strengthens them and makes them more unpredictable and dangerous outside of the Open Forum. That's the reason why we supported the neo-Nazis to come.

Instead of polarizing issues, she published a most wonderful article on that forum and covered more of the whole truth by including dialogue between the different sides at the forum. She did not say much about herself, but was as fair as possible toward all sides. Many reporters have become reporters because they are interested in social change. Don't let them remain invisible ghosts.

Answers to Media Questions about the Forum

Trying to answer the following questions may help you prepare for and conclude an Open Forum and/or deal with your own internal critic afterward. Here are some of the questions Amy and I have had to

142

deal with over time, in various places, and how we answered those questions.

Did your forum work? One answer is to ask the question, "What do you mean by *work?*" If the measure of success is speed, peace, and numbers, then yes and no! The road to peace opens quickly in large Open Forums. Amazing results sometimes happen almost instantly. However, peace is a process; it takes time; it takes large-group work. Peace takes relationship work and individual innerwork! Some of the examples mentioned already in this interview indicate how addressing serious tensions alleviates further distress in cities and organizations.

How about financial success? Yes, if the fair distribution of material rights is an issue, then organizations we have worked for, including Aboriginal groups, increase their material possessions and rights. In this sense, Open Forums "work." Less tension in organizations improves the working atmosphere and inevitably has good effects on the financial situation of everyone involved.

But please don't forget another question about success: "Did the community learn about itself?" To this question, the answer is "Always." Open Forums are 100 percent successful in revealing more parts of the community to its members.

What good are awareness and self-discovery in the end? The doubt in the back of this question is that the Open Forum self-discovery process does not produce immediate material results. The material level of consensus reality and the feeling level of Dreaming are linked. One does not hold without the other.

Yet, awareness itself can only be one drop in a large bucket. Filling that bucket is everyone's job, all the time. An Open Forum that lasts two hours is but one drop. If success is measured as filling a bucket, then a forum that puts one more drop into a bucket of water succeeds. If the forum's fire kindles someone's candle, then there is more light in that city or organization.

However, to a doubter who hates conflict, and who feels that self-discovery is too difficult, you can also say, "No, Open Forums are not successful in terms of always being pleasant." They never try to keep people quiet and or stop them from bringing up difficult topics and issues. Self-discovery can often be very disconcerting at first, even disturbing.

However, if group process was practiced with kids from earliest child-hood in schools, such Open Forums would be easier when people became adults.

Discovering the Media as a Big Dream

To get closer to the media as part of yourself and to test my theory that the media is a big dream, try the following innerwork.

1. Imagine picking up a newspaper and reading an incredible headline, any headline that comes to you. In your imagination, what does that headline say? For example, one of my readers imagined the following: Open Forum Accomplishes Miracle Reconciliation over Abuse of Power!

2. Now imagine the story beneath the headline. Write a few lines of the story now. For example, the above reader reported the following: One side said it was no longer interested in debate because it had been hurt enough and wanted immediate change. Very few from the other side came, but they insisted there was no problem. Finally, an amazingly detached older woman stood up and said remarkable things that made sense and healed the split, at least for today.

3. Now try to recall a recent dream. What was that dream? Write it down. For example, the above reader dreamed that "the Dalai Lama came to town."

4. Compare the "media" story with this dream. What does the story give you that the dream does not? For example, my reader said: "The Dalai Lama must be the spirit behind the older woman in the 'media' story. Interestingly the dream does not help me to understand its meaning within the content of my life, but the media story does. It says that someone like the Dalai Lama is needed in everyday life to solve a conflict I have with self-abuse. I needed that older woman and the Dalai Lama, so to speak, to understand the significance of both sides, instead of favoring one over the other!"

5. In what way are you sleeping in everyday life? Look at the "head-lines" in your story. Are they describing important events about your inner life of which you are not quite conscious? For exam-

ple, my reader wrote: "Yes. My dream and my story are trying to awaken me with big names like 'Dalai Lama, Winner of the Nobel Peace Prize.' That's me! The 'splash' produces big images so that I will take the new changes trying to happen inside of myself more seriously."

6. What is the larger context of the dream and the headline? What is the world and lifetime behind that story? For example, the reader had been depressed about her work, not realizing that some new philosophy beyond everyday life was occurring. This was big news for her.

I hope this innerwork gives you the sense that there is a great deal behind the media besides its overt representation—the way in which the newspapers, radio, and TV occupy the "media role." The role of the media is only partly occupied by the mass media. Other aspects of that role are in our dreams. There are many levels to the media. The point is that we are all responsible for filling the media's role and creating new stories and big dreams.

Things to Remember

1. The media is to the world as a big dream is to a sleeping person. The media asks you for sound bites and makes you feel more important than the rest of your community.

2. Become aware of all viewpoints within yourself instead of being polarized by the media and confronted with the good/bad, success/failure viewpoints.

3. The media takes problems out of context. Appreciate the story it is trying to tell but bring it back into context, reminding everyone of the larger goals and the forum's historical background.

4. Dialogue and subtle feeling changes do not make money. Good and evil are simpler than subtle awareness. Yet process is where important, immeasurable changes slowly (and sometimes rapidly) occur.

5. If you are passive relative to the media, you will see it as evil and yourself as good. However, if you choose to be active, you can use your own dualistic thinking to create your own story.

6. Write out your own story of what you imagine could—or

should—happen in your organization or city. This is the story that is driving you.

7. The whole truth includes subtlety and dialogue, as well as the personality and standpoint of the reporter. No one is only a role. *Who* that reporter is belongs in the story.

8. Did that forum work? Yes, always, in terms of increased awareness. If all it did was to announce and advertise its occurrence, it was a success.

CHAPTER 10

The Flu Shot against War

No one likes to be in a troubled business, a school that is tyrannized by some, or an organization that hurts people. However, because we know little about it, or see the process in simple terms of good and irreconcilably bad people, we all contribute to the tension, the war between the sides.

You might take a preventative flu shot if you want to avoid getting the flu. The flu shot works by giving you a little bit of the flu. Through that little bit of the flu you get in the shot, your body learns to protect itself against more flu. The same holds true for organizational trouble, war, and violence. Open Forums tend to prevent violence by giving folks a little bit of the potential trouble in the form of energetic discussion. Through that little bit of the problem, the communal body learns to protect itself against more trouble.

Just as people who cannot tolerate even the mildest symptoms of the little flu do not get a shot and may later get the big flu instead, cultures that will not tolerate intense Open Forum dialogues—and that means most cultures—suffer from violence, and later war. The point of my analogy is that war does not occur out of a clear blue sky. It takes *time* to create a war. When there is war against war, so to speak, and tension is neglected, it turns into enmity; when enmity is neglected, it turns to violence and war.

Right now there is plenty of violence worldwide. Kids everywhere from marginalized communities commit one form of suicide or another. Mainstream kids kill one another as never before. Scarcely a month goes by in the United States, for example, when some group is not "at war" with another, leaving behind injured and slain bodies. Where are the Open Forums?

War could easily become obsolete. However, it requires grassroots movements. Remember Vietnam. Remember how South Africa's grassroots movement changed everything, including the American government's policy toward the South African government. Remember the labor movements and the Civil Rights movement. Remember the Velvet Revolution in the former Czechoslovakia. Reforms in economic policies followed on the heels of these movements.

War Requires Your Utmost

We need to remember that for many, nothing is as exciting as war. To stop war, we must understand that it gives many a reason for living. In war, we can be heroes even if we cannot be one in everyday life. In war, we can be shamans, since we must use extrasensory intelligence to save ourselves and our own and to destroy the troublemakers. War is a chance for revenge. We need everything we have to create war. We can use it to prove ourselves and our lives worthwhile. Now beat all that!

The Open Forum beats all that. Worldwork, adapted to the Open Forum, has been used around the world in the midst of war zones and areas of severe conflict. It is my hope that the Open Forum will be used in the future as a method of avoiding severe conflict by having some conflict, letting it be, and finding the resolutions within the events themselves. I hope that the Open Forum will be used as a method of dealing with tension, once it has been recognized.

The first step for a facilitator working in the midst of areas of severe conflict or war zones is to acknowledge, to begin with, that "today it is you, tomorrow me." Today the people here look crazed and cannot give up their desire for revenge, but tomorrow, I could be crazed as well. Anyone can get lost in revenge.

The reason I stress the need for the facilitator to connect with his or her inner war-zone populace is because many facilitators who are not living in the midst of the war zone cannot understand why people will not let go of their history and stop retaliating. People in conflict seem crazy, mad. In part, this view is a projection of one's own unsolved problems at home.

Very few places on Earth are violence free; the potential for seeking revenge and retaliation can be found in just about everyone. We have competitive life-and-death struggles, gender battles, racial and religious conflicts everywhere. Just look at the town you live in, or the city nearest you. Look back in your own life, and look at your present life, look at the people you think you are "better than." Then you know war is not just in one place. In fact, any war is everyone's war.

Theories of War

When I was a child, kids were crippled by polio. Today, no one gets that disease anymore because there is a vaccination to prevent the virus from gaining a foothold. My theory is that the existence of any war means that the whole world has not solved the problem of war; it has not prevented the virus of hatred from gaining a foothold. Therefore, the problem of one war in one area means a world war for me.

In the Balkans during the war between the Serbs and the Albanians in Kosovo, the United States bombed the Serbs, accusing them of ethnic cleansing, of destroying the Albanians. One evening during that war, President Clinton declared on TV, after a mass shooting in a high school in Colorado, "America must teach its young to solve its problems without guns!" On the one hand, he bombed others, while on the other hand, he advocated just the opposite. That's our world. There is no such thing as a war in one area. We live in a world where the two hands of any given political leader are at war with themselves.

War was on my mind while I was writing this chapter. Staff members of a Norwegian government journal for policy-makers asked us for help in creating a viable peace treaty in Kosovo. They reminded us of what they had achieved a few years ago in the Middle East in the so-called "Oslo Peace Accord." Their journal was exploring why their methods were now failing in Kosovo. They had tried Jimmy Carter's method (which, by the way, was referred to as a "process-oriented method of conflict resolution"). Now they wanted to know what we thought about war.

Before explaining my own ideas about war, I want to summarize some war theories to show where mine fits in. First, let us define war as a violent, large-scale national and/or international conflict in which countries condone murder. Individual acts of violence can be understood as versions of war with fewer people and localities involved. Both exert physical force with the intent of injuring and killing people. The global and the individual situation are very closely linked.

Several theories on the origins of war follow:

Nationalism. Some political theories of war are centered on the concept of national *identity* as the essential variable in the creation of war. A given nation (or group) has an identity that needs to be respected, and if respect from another country is withheld, we have the beginnings of war—simmering hostility.

For example, World War II began, in part, because of Germany's humiliation from the earlier Treaty of Versailles following World War I. This humiliation left the populace vulnerable to the kind of "salve" Hitler offered: a war to prove their superiority and, at the same time, "cleanse" the world of undesirable human beings. Humiliation and injury play a role in war, just as they are core issues in individual acts of violence.

Capitalism. It is said that war makes money for people in capitalist countries. War-related technology research and production create work, and improve the economy. Powerful nations make money from war by selling planes, guns, computers, etc. So "war makes sense" economically, although gains are usually short-term and eventually disastrous to people and the environment. Nonsocial forms of capitalism focus on the financial gain of individuals and groups. The theory goes that economic benefits for the few who make weapons fuel tension between them and the public, as well as between the country and other nations.

Biology. This theory contends that human beings have the genetics of monkeys; we are as aggressive as our evolutionary predecessors. Biologists explain war biologically. We are possessed and programmed by the warrior instinct, and this is what causes war.

The need for the military. Military theories view the military as the defining element of a country. A powerful country is one with a lot of warriors. The more power you have, the better off you are. To be secure, you need a powerful military to protect you. Having a military is like having a weapon. You start looking for an enemy to shoot at.

"Shadow" factors. Some psychological theories of war are closely aligned with the biological view when they contend that war is due to the fact that men are aggressive and like to beat up other men. Another theory of war draws on the Jungian concept of the "shadow," which refers to that part of ourselves that we dislike and disown by projecting it onto other people, whom we then look down on. Projecting our "shadow" or the "dark part" of ourselves (an unwittingly racist psychological description of people) "out there," is the genesis of war.

Religion. Some theories say that war erupts because people don't respect the Great Spirit. Instead of believing something like "Thy will be done," people in war feel "My will be done." Some groups say, "War is due to past karma." Nonbelievers counter that religion itself is the cause of war.

Peacefulness. The war theory I have stressed in many parts of this book is that peacefulness itself is used as a paradigm to counteract tension. Being peaceful is seen as better than being in conflict. Thus, peace conflicts with conflict and thereby precipitates and amplifies existing tensions and creates the basis for war and ongoing battles.

To these various theories I would like to add what I label Fear of Dreaming: Fear of Large Diverse Groups.

Fear of Dreaming:
Fear of Large Diverse Groups

Most war theories do not suggest working with the entire system or with the holographic sections of systems found in Open Forums. The resistance against systems thinking is not theoretical, however; the fear

151

is due to lack of familiarity with large diverse groups in conflict, to lack of connection to dreaming.

Anger. Instead of working with the anger that is absolutely central to conflict of any kind, most theories try to stop it or explain it away. Many modern mediators and negotiators even send people out of the room if they get angry! We need to change our minds about anger and realize it is not difficult to work with. Most anger arises in response to not being heard, respected, or trusted. Therefore, listening, respecting, and trusting are the keys—and they are cost-free.

Multidimensional features of violence and war. Large-group work must be simultaneously coupled with personal inner and relationship work. We have had good experiences in riot and war zones doing large-group work, mixed with or followed by relationship work (see my *Sitting in the Fire*) between conflicting parties and innerwork. I cannot go into detail on the necessary methods in this present book, but only paint the larger picture—which includes awareness of *rank* and *power* in large groups, in relationships, in families, and inside the individual as well.

Rank awareness plays a crucial role in all violence in groups, relationships, and individuals. For example, teenagers become violent when they are rejected by their peers and feel like outcasts. Race as a ranking factor plays a role in "outcasting" people. Those with less athletic ability, physical power, consensual physical attractiveness, or intelligence are often treated with less respect and regarded as having less value, making them feel rejected and retaliatory.

We all need more rank awareness and consciousness of our own inner states of revenge and retaliation. My book *Sitting in the Fire* contains more tips for working on these topics.

All theories of violence have a piece in the picture. To see the whole picture, however, we need to consider all theories simultaneously. We cannot separate one issue or approach from another. For example, while working on nationality factors that contribute to violence, we must remember economics. While working on economics, we must remember race and gender. While working on sexism we have to remember health issues. While working on health issues we have to remember sexual orientation. While working on sexual orientation we have to remember racism.

We need multileveled awareness. While considering social issues, we must remember biology and genetics, the warrior instinct, and appreciate the diversity in religious viewpoints as well.

Think of an airplane. To design an airplane you need to know how high it must fly. You have to know about the effects on the plane of gravity, altitude, and velocity. You must calculate the power of the engine. Better keep the air pressure constant inside the plane; the structure must be solid. A radar system is needed to check on air traffic. Think about the temperature in the plane. Make sure pilots don't fall asleep. If you miss just one factor, the plane might crash.

The same principle holds for large communities: if you focus only on one or two issues, the community crashes. If you forget one factor, the plane will go down. If you focus on gun control but forget rank awareness, you still have murder. All factors need to be thought about and coordinated all the time.

In my group work with schools, businesses, communities, cities, and national issues, I recommend that someone or some group be selected to coordinate awareness of the various factors. The leaders, like the public, think that the problems with the world are due to one factor alone—to economics, or to the war instinct, or to the "shadow," or to the other aggressive nations. However, a wide-awake facilitating coordinator says, "Don't forget all the other factors, such as large group and individual consciousness!" That is the message of the multileveled, psychosocial activist seeking to facilitate simultaneous awareness of factors and levels, etc. The activist knows that if there is violence *anywhere*, we are not working together everywhere.

The world needs awareness coordinators to facilitate the process of working together. Groups of people working together, each with their own expertise, can solve the problem of violence in a community. I know this, because I have seen how large Open Forums reduce violence.

If one of the reasons war excites us is that we are challenged to our maximum, then let's make ordinary life as challenging. Try relationship work with someone you don't like! Solving that problem requires at least as much effort as trying to make peace when there is war.

War as an umbrella. In working with groups in Open Forums during wartime, fury, anger, and violence are imminent because they are ghosts. War is the umbrella reminding everyone of their worst abuse issues. It reminds us of the hurt, the fights, and the violence in our personal histories. One war reminds us of all wars.

During the war in the Balkans, our group in Portland held an Open Forum to explore why the United States intervened in Kosovo. Nonlinearity was the rule. Though the facilitators tried to hold the focus to this particular war in question, it was impossible. Koreans complained about Japanese invasions in World War II. Old Civil War conflicts arose between the U.S. participants. Unresolved enmity was mentioned between the United States and Germany, and between Poland and Russia.

War reminds us of the unsettled, internal agony within ourselves. Many in the United States are oblivious to wars outside this country because war has not been experienced on our soil since the Civil War (assuming we ignore the ongoing ethnic conflicts and the "war" with the Native Americans). However, another reason why people can become oblivious to the realities of war is that they are oblivious to—or choose to ignore—the conflicts in their own families. Thus, when war breaks out somewhere, everyone is shocked, even though conflict is imminent just about everywhere in personal life.

Violence is an extreme state. Trying to cajole people experiencing hatred, anger, and violence into a more tractable, normal state of consciousness by suggesting good-heartedness or nonviolence rarely works for long. Recall the forum in Dublin I mentioned earlier in this book. Telling the combatants to cool down did not help; what *did* help was awareness.

I prefer to frame violence as an extreme state of consciousness and to deal with it as such. One way of dealing with extreme states is to join them. Joining someone in a violent, dangerous state and saying, "YES! Please understand where 'we' are coming from," has ameliorating effects, if done spontaneously and genuinely.

I remember during one Open Forum I joined in with an Asian person who began screaming and threatening to walk out of room. She was almost incomprehensible, she was so angry at other Asian nations for denigrating her country. As she screamed, I stood next to her and joined her in demanding: "We want respect, we want our issues to be heard, and no one has listened. Understand that we are furious and violent not just because we are angry people, but because of past hurt. Yes, we seek revenge, but we want more than just revenge. Do not put us down for being angry. Remember the pain of history. I am screaming to be heard and escalate the situation because the rest of the world sits around and does nothing, just as many of you sit around feeling smug!"

As I continued to voice what I imagined to be behind her momentary extreme state with genuine passion (drawing on my own experiences of fury when I feel unheard), she calmed down and listened. I went on. "If you had lived through what I have lived through, you would not be so smug. You would understand that I want a better world, a world where atrocities such as I have been through will no longer happen. I want a better world!" She calmed down and affected those who had been "smug."

Feeling into "mainstream" power. As soon as I was done with her side, I wondered, how could I feel more deeply into the mainstream folks who had just been accused of smugness? The message of that side was "Who wants to deal with all this war stuff? My personal life is okay the way it is. Let me be!" These people have the good luck and the privilege to ignore situations in their immediate environments; they can sit back, watch TV, and channel surf.

How do you deal with the part of the world that feels, "Oh, this is too much, I don't want to think about it?" There are all sorts of ways of dealing with that. Some people throw bombs, others commit terrorists attacks. Another way is to join the mainstream folks in their space by feeling your way into the "smug" position, which is really a fear of anger and conflict. Perhaps at the essence of this side is the feeling, "I don't want to take sides, I want to be neutral and peaceful and merely criticize others." As a facilitator, you can support this side of the community as well by framing the desire to step outside the conflict as a desire to be centered, peaceful, and neutral.

Help them step outside and value peace. Perhaps use it to help others work on their conflicts! Help the peace lovers understand that they should not make "war" by feeling they are superior to those who are upset and express themselves more emotionally. Absence of emotion is often a form of behavior assumed by those of greater economic, social, and/or spiritual rank. But *true rank* would understand that as long as we are in the human form, we are all as much fire as water.

I think of neutral nations and how they attempt to stay out of war. Such countries and individuals could have incredible power to help other places in the world. However, those with such immense privileges—those with the privilege to choose peace and quiet—are not using their neutrality as a vehicle for fostering positive developments. In a recent interview with a leading Swiss newspaper, I suggested Switzerland use its professed neutrality to study and develop conflict resolution procedures and become proud of itself as a facilitator between nations (instead of acting neutral while using war to make money). In addition, all of those who have the privilege to lead peaceful lives might hold an Open Forum (or course) in the workplace and family.

As a facilitator in an Open Forum, care for those with privilege and power; they have positions that can be aligned with your work to render war obsolete. In fiery debates, they need to be remembered too. Care for them by understanding them and joining them when they are attacked and unable to defend themselves. Remember that *people* are not *roles*.

Try taking a mainstream role and saying, "Those of us who are mainstream people usually don't identify with having social rank and power. We are just learning about these things that we take for granted. Now we understand that we can use our privilege to help others."

If you do not help people from marginalized positions who want revenge to reframe their position as looking for a better world, then retaliation against the mainstream takes over during the Open Forum and even afterward in the form of terrorism. When war and violence become imminent in the forum, step into the marginalized position and explain the sense of hatred and revenge, then switch sides to express the feelings of the mainstream as well.

Once both sides have been represented, a moment arises when *growing together* becomes possible: It is this growing together that is the seed to a more peaceful world. Whenever war is the issue, the polarized positions are often avoiding conflict on one side and grief and frustration on the other. Without facilitation, frustration leads to anger, rage, and retaliation. Again, if you can feel into both sides and articulate them, growing together happens. *The solution to war is not peace but growing together.*

When this growing process begins, the side that has been marginalized begins to remember long-forgotten and painful memories about war. That pain, which everyone wanted to forget, rises out of the past like the spirit of the dead. As a facilitator, you need to hear and grieve that history, present now. Go into the history, not around it. There you find the hope for a better future. Even ask the dead what kind of world they would create today. The dead can be wiser than the living. I remember forums in Europe where the dead spoke for the first time, asking the living to learn from history. The exception is if you are working in an area where violence or war has just abated. In that case, people may even need help avoiding such subjects in an Open Forum, where gentleness and patience are needed.

We have met terrorists from different sections of the world who have spent their lives fighting for their cause and who have killed other people. The "killers" told us that their sense of retaliation was only the beginning; at the core of the retaliation was a deep need to remind the other side of the agony of the past that has become the present because it was ignored. History is a ghost that hovers here, now, today. In addition, the agony will not stop if its essence is not expressed: "Please remember we are not just retaliating; behind our anger is a search for equality."

It's true that revenge is momentarily sweet, but even sweeter yet is the awesome process leading to equality and relationship. I know this from working with people who have killed others. Those who attacked mainstream people are trying to remind the so-called mainstream folks of their own repressed agony. The teleology of such attacks is to bring back into awareness everyone's experiences of having been ignored and the resulting marginalized feelings of anger and violence. Many people in mainstream positions cut themselves off from these feelings in order to continue living in a certain manner. Acknowledging one's own extreme states is not simple, but the sense of relief makes it all worthwhile.

Open Forums and living theater. I suggest holding televised Open Forums and using facilitators who understand these agonized states of mind. Show such forums around issues of violence to the media in violence-prone areas. Process the intensity of war between opposing parties on radio, TV, and e-mail. Do this everywhere violence is impending. It can help.

If you process the sides of an issue on TV—and in other electronic media in front of everybody—there is a chance that the people at war, the people who are watching, will feel understood. When people feel seen and represented, there is relief.

This reminds me of a gay man I met on the street corner in down-town Portland one day while I was jogging with Amy. We had just facilitated an Open Forum on television between gay activists and a Christian group opposed to gay rights. There had been violence between the groups, and both sides were terrified. To make the story short, the Open Forum succeeded in getting to the common ground between the two groups: fear of being beaten and hope for a safer future. The scene was very moving and was picked up by local and public TV stations. On the street, he said hello, and thanked us for the work our whole community had done to make a safer life for him and his friends. Amy and I were very touched, but what was more important, we realized how crucial was the portrayal of that Open Forum on TV. In the past, theater acted out our cultural problems and had healing effects on a community. Theater is important. It gives us a chance to see our issues enacted.

The bottom line? Begin at home. Encourage your family, your organization, your town, and your city to be proud of its differences and to discuss them openly. Do not submerge the diversity, especially if violence is about to erupt.

In a tense school situation, bring out the diversity and tensions between the so-called athletes and the "outcasts." Show differences in ability, in rank, in social status. *Show* revenge. *Understand* retaliation. Have compassion for anger. In businesses, bring up the problems before they disturb everyone. Create "Playback Theatre"; show and remind everyone about what happened. Laugh and cry together.

War and enlightenment. War can be an enlightenment process. War is so terrible that it almost forces us to rediscover healing poetry, love, and forgiveness. Songs such as "For Whom the Bell Tolls," "Where Have All the Flowers Gone," and "Dona, Dona, Dona" remind us of the ineffable. I have always been touched by a song sung by a man on the way to his death in a concentration camp:

On a wagon bound for market
There's a calf with a mournful eye
High above him there's a swallow
Winging swiftly through the sky.
How the winds are laughing
They laugh with all their might
Laugh and laugh the whole day through
And half the summer's night.
Dona, Dona, Dona, Dona.

"Stop complaining," says the farmer
"Who told you a calf to be?
Why don't you have wings to fly with?
Like that swallow, proud and free?"
(Chorus)
Calves are easily bound and slaughtered
Never knowing the reason why
But whoever treasures freedom
Like the swallow will learn to fly.
—Aaron Zeitlin, 1940

This song is both beautiful and difficult. It is hard to see the image of a human being having to accept her being led to slaughter, like a calf with a mournful eye. It makes us shudder. From another viewpoint, the viewpoint of the bird, the swallow learning to fly, the song says the winds are laughing while below the cattle are being led away. The nearness of death and the unfairness of war intersect in divine insight in this songwriter. The winds remain unaffected and the bird flies free and can see the animal about to be slaughtered "never knowing why." Yet, "whoever treasures freedom . . . will learn to fly." I think also of a passage in the Bhagavad-Gita of the incredible discussion between warrior Arjuna and the divine Krishna on the battlefield on the eve of the war. Krishna speaks of detachment from all worldly involvement.

It has been my hope that now, without more war, we can learn from history that we are more than one side or the other. The unresolved suffering caused by hurt and its result, unrelenting retaliation, can only dissolve by detachment from one role or the other. Perennial spiritual wisdom teaches the same principle: detach from this world, this person, her successes, and failures.

Until now, such detachment meant nonviolence and the transcendence of the material plane. Now detachment can have another meaning. Detachment must no longer lead to disinterest in and disconnection from the world, but to a new kind of immersion in the Dreaming. This kind of immersion in conflicts, coupled with appreciation of all sides, can replace transcendence as a goal.

The Future of War

Today, I realize that my past hopelessness about the future of the world was partly due to having too little knowledge of the individuals who actually go to war. I used to look negatively at the world and its future. Now that I have had contact with freedom fighters and those who begin wars, I see new possibilities. In the past the world seemed just crazed and hopeless to me. Today I know that extreme states of consciousness are not just bombs ready to go off, but also invitations to explore the spirit of relationship, the factors binding us together as a human race and planetary biosystem.

Amazingly beneficial effects come from noticing signals, developing consciousness of rank and ghosts in large groups, and learning about oppression. Our human race is not simply unconscious or evil; given the chance, we can do differently. Don't sentence us to extinction by making war against war.

We need to learn how to work on contentious issues. We can do better than war by fostering deep democracy. The new kinds of awareness now afoot make war look old-fashioned. Most of the extreme states leading to war can be avoided. If you get to the root of your own and the "other's" anger, that is, if you feel into violence, you know that the agony will not dissipate if its essence is not discovered: "Please remember that we are not just retaliating; we are searching for equality."

Conflict work is a new kind of meditation hall, a place to learn awareness and to feel into all sides of the world and yourself. In some mysterious way, potential violence may have been needed to allow us a glimpse of the possible routes to freedom, and to find solutions to war.

Things to Remember

1. Any single war is a world war, since war stems from conflicts that are not addressed.

2. War theories marginalize working with diverse, large groups of conflicting contestants.

3. Open Forums model awareness in innerwork, relationship work, rank, and power at all levels and moments and thereby reduce violence.

4. To prevent violence and war, supplement working on one topic by working with awareness of all topics at the same time. Under the umbrella of one problem are all the others. While working on race, remember gender. While working on sexism, remember economics. While working on economics, remember dreaming, biology, military theory, etc.

5. Severe conflict challenges us to make everyday life more exciting and to risk processing contentious diversity issues on our own home front.

6. Join someone in a violent, dangerous state and say, "YES! I understand where 'we' are coming from," to ameliorate conflict.

7. If you feel into violence, you know that agony cannot dissipate if its essence is not discovered: "Please remember that we are not just retaliating, we are searching for equality."

8. Reduce world violence with moment-to-moment awareness of oppression. Once we recognize that processing social issues is one of the best meditation halls for enlightenment, we can develop awareness of all sides. Then we discover that potential violence is a path to outer equality and inner freedom.

9. With all this in mind, we can sigh deeply in relief as we recognize that war is now old-fashioned.

CHAPTER 11

The Open Forum as the Elder's Monastery

Fortunately, elders always seem to pop up wherever there are Open Forums. Perhaps they are that inevitable part of the organizational field that manages to rise above the troubles of the moment and care for the whole. Sometimes it seems as if they are responsible for helping the world go round.

When I first realized this some years ago, I made it a practice to interview such elders, asking them how they managed to do what they do. Most said something to the effect that they feel that the whole world was their child or their family. A particular feature characterizes such elders: at one time or another, they themselves have suffered from some sort of marginalization.

Most multicultural elders have been deeply hurt at one time or another—abused, shamed, or stripped of social power. In a way, this particular feature of having been hurt reminds me of C. G. Jung's image of the individual therapist as a "wounded healer"—that is, one who helps others because she has survived her own painful experiences. Like the shamans going through their training in aboriginal societies, the best Open Forum facilitators-elders have also been hurt. In a way, they have even died, in the sense of having detached a bit from their earlier identities. Multicultural elders may have been victims of oppression, but they learned to free themselves enough from the oppressed role to feel their way into other "spirits" in any given conflict. They seem to know all the sides, regardless of the issue.

Seeing them work is awesome. I remember an African American woman chuckling simultaneously to herself and to everyone else in the midst of a huge conflict around Latino rights in the southern part of the United States. Just when everything seemed deadlocked, when the various sides stood checkmated, face-to-face, frustrated and angry with one another, she just laughed and spoke.

"Look at this," she said to everyone. "Come on kids, just look at this!" she suggested. "This is the cost of democracy. It's not simple, but it's sure worthwhile!" She broke out into such infectious laughter, she transformed the contentious atmosphere. She then broke out in song: "We Shall Overcome." Some cried and everyone joined in with her. Three minutes later, everyone was laughing and working together!

During a tense Open Forum on the topic of racism (directed mainly against Aborigines) in Australia, a gay Jewish man came forward at one moment to help. At first, this Open Forum seemed to have been composed mainly of liberals fighting for Aboriginal rights. It looked as if the racists had all remained at home. Since no one had been able or willing to see their own racism, the racist became a ghost—who was not present. One speaker after another spoke about those the evil racists "out there" when this gay man stood up, telling everyone he was racist toward Aborigines.

He was obviously not the kind of bigot we normally associated with a prejudiced racist; he was neither obstinately nor intolerantly devoted to his own opinions or prejudices. Nevertheless, he explained that though he was both gay and Jewish, being from oppressed groups did not prevent him from being racist against others. He said he knew both the oppressor and the oppressed within his own life, when he was not being beaten for one thing then it was another. Yet being a member of marginalized groups did not make him perfect; he was still capable of being unconscious and unwittingly inflicting pain against others.

He spoke about how he would try—when possible—to forget the

suffering of others and to simply disappear into his own privileged light male skin. His statements fit just about everyone who was not Aboriginal, and may even have fit the innerwork of some Aboriginal people. He was clear and explicit about his own unwitting racism and, at the same time, supported the Aboriginal community. Though a man in his very early twenties, he was an elder—personal, honest, and caring for everyone at that Open Forum.

We are all thankful to those elders who almost magically appear when they are needed. The elder is a "participant-facilitator," an ordinary person who feels responsible for caring for all. The world is a scary place to be without them. However, when such an elder is present, the world becomes a guesthouse, a sort of "home" where just about everything and everyone seems to be welcome and somehow needed. Elders create an atmosphere for people and for the invisible spirits in the air whose lack of representation makes us humans nervous. In a way, Open Forum is their spiritual center, their monastery.

When elders are present, they turn their own experience of oppression into a gift for others. People hurt by their own families or who come from marginalized communities understand oppression because they have lived the details of it. In a way, seen within the context of the Open Forum, they have a kind of spiritual power and manage to facilitate the global scene by modeling generosity toward others. Within the confines of a given Open Forum, such people have rank— even though outside of that forum, in most sections of this world, they have less, and are likely to be kicked around for who they are.

How Elders Grow

If you have been put down by others, you are on the way to becoming an elder, whether or not you come from a marginalized community. You know one of the great truths about life, a truth that others try to forget. Everyone and anyone can abuse power unconsciously. No one is free from being unwittingly abusive to others. Moreover, abuse is not entirely an outer issue.

However, knowing these truths is only the beginning of working through oppression; it takes patience, time, and in some cases, cannot be completed in one lifetime. There may be years of numbness when you tried to forget the hurt. You were paranoid about others, or had fits of rage against certain kinds of people. Even if you never identified the discomfort of paranoia or rage as originating in acts of oppression against yourself, you may have suffered from depression or thoughts of revenge. You may have unconsciously sought comfort in smoking, or the compulsive use of drugs, alcohol, food, or sex. You may have become an excessive caretaker of others. Perhaps you developed other compulsions. Maybe you feared you were insane. Some people try to forget the pain by explaining that it is independent of personal history. Each of us has his or her own way of dealing with oppression.

Then comes another stage in awareness of oppression. After discovering that something was bothering you, you may have turned toward religion or spirituality to soothe the problems of this world. On the other hand, perhaps you joined gangs or became an intellectual to "get back." Emotionally exhausted from your own troubles, perhaps you decided to avoid the world altogether, or at least situations such as the Open Forum, where events threatened to remind you of the difficult past. Perhaps you even thought that those who get angry and talk about social issues are stupid.

You went through so many cycles of getting angry and depressed with the world that you began to let go of your anger, as if your fire had no more wood to burn. Perhaps "burning your wood" is what led you to become the elder that you are, capable of compassionate interest in the problems of others. Though perhaps you thought you could disappear from this mundane world of conflict, something brought you back.

The elder is not just an individual but a role in the group composed of individuals like yourself who may not always have realized that they are drawn in by the field of conflict to help. In other words, you are not only an elder, but, like the other group members, may be one of many who can occupy this role. When you don't occupy this role, others will step into it from your organization or city. The elder knows she is a person but also a role. She is aware that she is dispensable.

Eldership is the result of inner development and in response to outer circumstances. Because she knows that the field draws her in, she is some complex combination of mystic and activist, a part of everyone, connected to the suffering of her people and, at the same time, to the infinite.

Most of the elders I have met are not well known; in fact, most may never be known beyond their intimate group of friends and the moment in time in which they speak their wisdom in an Open Forum. Others are famous. I think of Nelson Mandela from South Africa, who has largely avoided polarizing blacks against whites so that the different peoples of his country can work together. I think of Mahatma Gandhi's leadership, Martin Luther King, Jr.'s spirituality, and the balance of his apparent teacher, the minister Howard Thurman, as well as many others. I marvel at the Dalai Lama's equanimity in the face of adversity within Tibet. I recall the history of Joan of Arc, that "simple maid of Orleans" (as she liked to call herself), who was burned at the stake before the age of twenty, but who succeeded in helping France to unify itself. With only spiritual power, she could do what kings could not!

By following their dreams, these elders remind us that great visions yearn to become real. The elder knows that not only is she herself a dream, but all groups are mythic, held together by ancient beliefs, traditions, spirits, and new stories. That is why the elder is a dreamer as well as a realist.

While the famous leaders model aspects of what is needed in working on global conflicts, we all need to value more highly the less visible elders. These less-apparent powers are the ones who hold the world together. They monitor the slow transition needed to help groups transform from self-destructive conglomerations of adversaries into co-creative communities proud of their interactive gatherings.

Every Day Is More Than a Fine Day

Because of their detachment, elders can be sweet and motherly, but also scary and unpredictable because of their awesomeness. An elder uses her awareness to see changes as they are trying to emerge. She notices her own emotional transitions and can move between the roles of facilitator, teacher, social activist, Zen master, and even criminal. For example, in one of his poems, the most compassionate Vietnamese

Buddhist priest, Thich Naht Hanh, says, "Call me the young woman who was raped, and the man who did it."

For the elder, switching roles is not a technique to be learned, but an ability that arises within her in response to the moment and for the benefit of all. Though she suffers the problems of the day with everyone else, you have the feeling that, in some uncanny way, whether the day is good or not is not her single goal. Selflessness is part of her teaching. She may have a very strong mind of her own and, at the same time, may act is if she has no self at all; rather, she is a channel through which nature speaks. She is active but, in a way, does nothing. I remember the words of the mystic Anasuya Devi from India, who said that no one can do anything, you can't help others. Nature does it all. Fill the role given to you (Conway 1994).

Because the elder knows that the Dreaming gives rise to the various experiences we have, she teaches that total awareness comes only from a whole community, not just from an individual, including herself. For her, this world is hell and heaven, a garbage can *and* a miracle. She manifests the second revolution by fighting for human rights and discovering the right to be free of any one particular human form.

Being Only Yourself Is a Problem

Perhaps because of her detachment, the elder knows that the dialogues that occur in Open Forums are both personal and impersonal. In fact, though others relate to her as if she were a person, she knows that to identify only with her name and her body is a kind of inner tyranny. In other words, it may be wonderful to be yourself—the self is an amazing construction of nature—but *always* being *only* yourself is a problem.

Sticking to your identity makes you fear change, which is the spirit of Dreaming. That is why most of us become terrified when we must face transitions from childhood to adulthood, to parenthood, to eldership, and finally to death. If you identify with your old identity, transitions are traumatic.

When you are an elder who knows that she and everything else changes, every group problem you encounter is connected with *your* changing. When you are not in the role of the elder, group problems seem foreign to you, and you are barely aware that the world's problems are related to your own static and frozen self. As long as your personal history prevails, the organic nature of role-switching—leaving one role and developing new ones—becomes impossible. However, when eldership prevails, you become a participant facilitator, edgeless and free. For you, freedom manifests as the truth in the various roles and the awareness experiences into and out of which you move.

The Elder's Mindlessness

A story about a friend of mine, Keido Fukushima from Kyoto, Japan, helps to illustrate the relativity of the self. One day we were talking about letting go of the self and the process of making "mistakes." I told him that process-oriented thinking considers accidental mistakes part of the Dreaming and potentially significant. He liked the basic idea that if I made a mistake, the Dreaming in nature is trying to express itself through me in that particular "mistake." By appreciating "mistakes," misfortune can become good fortune. He told me the following story, which I am relating from memory.

He was visiting San Francisco, several years ago, where he was asked to teach, using his special abilities as a calligrapher, an artist who uses stylized and elegant forms of handwriting, to demonstrate his ideas. When he arrived in San Francisco, however, he realized that he had forgotten his special calligraphy pen. Perhaps you are thinking, "How can a calligrapher forget his pen? That would be like a violinist forgetting his violin!" He told me that he'd thought such things as well.

In any case, realizing just two hours before his class was due to start that he had forgotten his calligraphy pen, he rushed to Chinatown, and ran into a shop that sold pens. He told the Chinese shopkeeper, "Please help, I need to buy a pen!" The shopkeeper stared at him for a moment and said: "I see from the special robes you are wearing that you must be a Zen master, perhaps a famous one. Dear Roshi, Zen master, how could you have forgotten your pen?"

My friend, who *is* a Zen master (and head of the Zen Buddhist Rinzai sect in Japan) said, "Yes, I forgot. Please sell me one pen." The

Chinese shopkeeper said, "Oh, you are a Zen master, how strange that you forget things!" and promptly sold him a new pen.

The next year the Roshi returned to San Francisco and, again, he forgot something. This time he missed his calligraphy paper, the long roles of parchment needed for his demonstration. What a bad moment to realize he had forgotten the paper! Again, two hours before the class, together with the disciples he travels with, he ran downtown to the same Chinese shop from the year before. This time, after he told the shopkeeper that he had forgotten his parchment and needed to buy some, the man could not help exclaiming: "Dear Roshi, dear Zen master. Last year you forgot your pen. This year you have forgotten paper. What will you forget next year?" and laughed.

The Roshi told us that the shopkeeper's question was like a deep *koan* (a question or paradox meant to forward enlightenment) for him. The *koan* set the Roshi into meditation. What would he forget next year? Then suddenly he got the answer. *Satori!* He said to the Chinese shopkeeper, "Next year what will I forget? *Next year I shall forget the calligrapher!*" And with that, he, Amy, and I burst out laughing so hard, tears rolled down our cheeks.

If there is a single Zen teaching—which, of course, there is not—it would be, "forget yourself." Most of us think that when we make mistakes, we have failed at something. However, in forgetting the pen and the paper, the Roshi found a truth: forget the calligrapher! It is not easy to translate his Zen teachings from Japanese into English. *Ho-ge-jaka Ji-yu* means approximately that the self on which you depend can be discarded. Now that does not mean that we have no self; it rather suggests that we depend less on our primary process, our identity, and allow an open, creative "Zen-mind." If you have Zen mind, the hand moves and a picture is painted, yet there is no painter. That is one reason why Fukushima Roshi uses calligraphy to demonstrate Zen.

He told us this story while we were sitting together in his monastery in Kyoto surrounded by beautiful gardens and magnificent trees. It was then that I noticed an unwanted thought attracting my attention; I was jealous of him. I saw him sitting in this wondrous monastery, which looks relatively peaceful, while at that time, Amy and I were sitting in the fire of the outer world with all its fury and hatred. (Actually, he too travels widely dealing with a public, often full of conflict—but I was not remembering all that in the moment of my projection and jealousy.)

I told him about the path Amy and I are following and about recent Open Forums. He spontaneously said, "That path is a good path!" This meant to me that each of our paths was valuable and, at the same time, also just a path. I thought of Castaneda's learning from his shaman teacher Don Juan that everyone's path leads to the same place—nowhere.

Death of the Facilitator

Today I understand that the real world of ours that is full of peace and conflict *is* a monastery. I love the peacefulness and beauty of identified monasteries, but I also realize that peace is a state of mind that can be found anywhere we go. At that time, I needed more of a sense of detachment in my self and my work, the detachment I projected onto the Roshi. My *koan* was "Forget the facilitator and become one." That is, "Become an elder." Or said differently, "Let things happen!"

After training yourself and learning as much as you can, it is time to let the facilitator go, let her die, let her move aside for nature to take her place. The facilitator's symbolic death is a paradoxical moment in which you are both dead and alive at the same time. When the facilitator is forgotten, the elder arises, and things happen on their own. At that moment, the Open Forum, social dialogue, and organizational development become nature's artwork. When the facilitator becomes an elder, the Open Forum transforms into a monastery in which our interactions become nature's painting.

Mindlessness in Relationship

As a facilitator, you know that group work is a matter of suffering, life, and death. However as an elder, you realize that freedom, equality, and civil rights are attainable only with detachment and awareness of Dreaming. Nature's artwork is dramatic. Let her theater unfold; portray her hidden signals and ghosts, subtle feelings and monsters, devils and goddesses, the oppressors and the oppressed. Leave your everyday self. Forget yourself—at least, now and then—so that nature can use you to paint with.

Be mindless in relationships in the sense of switching sides and roles as your awareness reveals changes. *Mindlessness* means your everyday mind realizes that it does not know for certain who anyone (including yourself) really is. Since we are all essentially mysteries in the midst of transformation, you will never really know who the "other" is. Here are a few tips on how to do this:

> Facilitate conflict around issues of diversity and international tension by using mystical experience and the roles of everyday life.
>
> Let town meetings in cities and organizations become Taoist monasteries connecting individual psychology with world problems.
>
> Let the work be simple. Give the power of change back to Nature. Then you know world events mirror your innerwork and your innerwork is political.
>
> Practice all this in your next face-to-face and cyberspace contact.
>
> Practice, then forget it.

Things to Remember

> 1. Elders rise above the troubles of the moment, care for the whole, and experience the world as their family. A particular feature characterizes these people: they have learned to heal themselves from the deep wound of being shamed or stripped of social power.
>
> 2. People from marginalized communities know the details of oppression. In the Open Forum they have more spiritual power and, in principle, are better able to facilitate and educate others. Within the context and social setting of Open Forums, such people can change the world.
>
> 3. The elder is a mystic in action, a person connected to the suffering of her people and to something infinite and timeless. She can bring perennial wisdom to bear on the anguish of the moment.

4. After training, do your best as a facilitator. When you are exhausted, let the facilitator "die." Let her go. That paradoxical moment allows the elder to be born and for nature to direct us.

5. From the elder's perspective, the Open Forum—which seems like hell to the ordinary state of mind—is a monastery. She sees the world as a sacred place where all events contribute to strengthening the sense of a community of all beings.

6. Relationships and community are calligraphy, strokes painted by nature. Seeing this frees you to let the brush paint the picture according to the dreaming of the moment.

7. Let go of your everyday mind. Enter the Dreaming. Then you know life itself is but a dream waiting to be discovered and lived.

Keys to the Open Forum

Our world is on the verge of remembering deep feelings. Some people are beginning to realize that the same oppressive ghosts that marginalize and disenfranchise groups marginalize the Dreaming as well. These are the same ghosts that spook us inside our hearts, trouble our communities, organizations, and countries. This incredible, wonderful, and terrifying world of ours is a dream theater. Our world is far more complex than our present view of reality allows. We are all on stage: you, me, and the ghosts of tyranny, self-dislike, love, and God. Social transformation involving freedom and equality happens in a sustainable manner by freeing communities and individuals— every person—to dream and process this theatre outside and inside. In a way, whether or not our organizations and this world become awesome and safe communities depends on your awareness and your becoming a participant-facilitator.

Keys to the Open Forum

Take the following keys with you to the forum to help unlock its potential.

PART I.

Conducting the Open Forum:

Learning the Fundamentals

A. Beyond the Rules of Order:
Extend democracy into deep democracy

1. Democracy is based on power. Without awareness, democracy adds to, but does not resolve, world problems.

2. Typical democratic procedures, such as *Robert's Rules of Order*, rule in favor of efficiency over feelings.

3. If "Robert" is not clearly noticed, respected, and described as a spirit in the room, any meeting is bound to be as repressive as it is efficient.

4. Deep democracy is a new awareness procedure that respects all individuals, parts, and states of consciousness.

B. The Open Forum as Outer and Innerwork: The background and meaning of the gathering

1. If you strive to do too much, you may be relying on the use of power instead of awareness. Insecurity occurs if you try to do something without *feeling* inspired. We don't need you as a leader for world change. Change is inherent in people and nature. You need awareness, not power, to notice and follow the changes.

2. If you are afraid, use your fear as a role in the process. Your role can lead to greater caring and more respect. In fact, your fear (or courage) can be just what your organization is denying or marginalizing. The organization needs *you, with all your fears*, to lead Open Forums—without changing your basic nature. You don't have to act more courageous than you are. Your own personality is a key to conflict work.

3. One of the goals of the Open Forum is to gain a vivid sense of the nongovernmental power I call "We, the people." The Open Forum has, in a way, the power to solve the hopelessness problem.

4. Open Forums give individuals hope by creating the chance for large groups to directly impact the media and the powers that govern us. We need to remember that grassroots groups initiate political changes in the world!

5. The Open Forum shows how to stop abuse from taking place in a given moment on a person-to-person level, which is something a government is not able to do. It doesn't know how to do that. It can only make rules: it cannot *make* people become conscious of their actions and their consequences.

6. Be clear about your personal goals. Do you want global peace? Do you want to be known better? Do you have a social activist goal/position and want to change a part of the community? Be clear about your goals, then explore the degree to which your goals intersect with those in the community as a whole. Who does and does not share your goals? How do your

goals coincide with, or differ from, those of the people who are coming to the forum? If you are not clear about the possible one-sided nature of your goals, your community may become your opponent.

7. If someone outside your own organization has hired you to do an Open Forum, be clear about his or her motives. Whom are they fighting? Who is the "other" for them? "Other" may be one of the roles you need to represent when the time comes.

8. To lay a solid foundation of inner awareness and clarity, conduct an imaginary Open Forum as if all the players and their opposing viewpoints represent aspects of yourself.

C. The Open Forum as Groupwork: Whom to invite, where to have it, when to begin

1. If only one person in one hundred is aware of what is happening, the group will feel safe and respected.

2. Today you may look crazy. Tomorrow, it could be me. Therefore, "You today and me tomorrow" is my motto. It could also be "Me today and you tomorrow."

3. After discovering your personal goals, you need to ask the community members about their goals. Are they interested in feeling safer? Do they want a greater sense of community? What are their diversity issues? The economic issues? Know the history of the topic and the history of the people involved.

4. For your own clarity, create a story, a myth, for that organization (or town), that incorporates everyone's story. Tell the story to others to check its validity.

5. Any given organizational issue is just a label; it is also a crucial label, the one troubling your group just now. At the same time, the label is an *umbrella* covering subsidiary issues that are intimately connected to the issue being discussed. You need to know the subsidiary issues; otherwise, they will arise and detract from the main issue.

6. How has the community dealt with the topic and issues in the past? Find out about present open community methods and programs. Network and collaborate with these programs, your present work can benefit from and build on existing methods.

7. Now that you know about the issue, *name your Open Forum*. If you want to hold a town meeting with all relevant groups present, it is best to choose a name for the forum that is inclusive, not exclusive.

8. Speak with the trusted elders of the groups involved on various sides of the issue. Elders are not just the bosses; they are folks, young or old, who are respected by their communities. Meet with as many of them as you can ahead of time. Consider inviting the elders to sit with you.

9. Location and timing make a difference. Choose a location and a time that foster inclusiveness.

10. Advertising is important. Create a warm invitation, friendly and personal. Be clear about the information you include in the invitation and follow it. When the forum begins, refer to that invitation; tell the folks again what the forum is about. In addition, do your legwork—calling people and asking them to come. Make sure they feel respected.

11. To feel more prepared, find out from your friends, acquaintances, and co-workers how you are seen publicly in terms of your age, race, gender, education, etc. Is the role people expect you to play the same role with which you identify?

12. Choose speakers from the most extreme positions you can find on the issue to avoid the "hovering ghosts" phenomenon.

13. Who has been a leader or elder in that group before? Be careful about turning against someone or some role that may be present at the forum. You need to be conscious of that role and help facilitate it at another point. Remember, each role is needed for the field to be complete, and people are not just people, but roles.

14. Adapt your work at the Open Forum to the community.

Find out about their belief system; situation (where are they today?); style (do they all talk at once, or one at a time, do they act politely, what's their language, cultural style, etc?); size (if there are ten members, you can take more time with each individual); time commitment (is this an ongoing group, or are they together for one night?). Develop your awareness, but stress *their* awareness.

15. Conduct mock forums. Prepare to work on issues ahead of time both in yourself and with teammates. In community work (including organizational development and town meetings), use deep democracy and work on your own feelings about the forum when doing a mock forum inside of yourself. This is inner worldwork. What atmosphere do you expect at the forum? What roles will be present? What ghosts? Are all these outer facts not also part of who you are?

D. The Facilitator's Awareness Work: Learn about roles, ghosts, and hot spots

1. When you are about to begin the Open Forum, take a minute and acknowledge the location you have chosen and the language you are using and how either or both factors might marginalize some participants.

2. Begin by introducing yourself; comment on your communication style and personality, the funny things about yourself, your fears, etc. If you don't speak about yourself right off the bat (but *keep it brief*), your audience will interrogate or even attack you at a later point.

3. Acknowledge suffering. Especially in tense conflict zones where there has been a lot of injury and loss, you need to acknowledge the enormity of the undertaking. Say something like, "We are going to hold an Open Forum on an issue that is very painful. Some people may not want to think about this issue, much less discuss it. That is why not everyone is here. Thanks to those of you who have come."

4. Thank elders and all others for coming, and thank your helpers. Mention the amount of time allotted for the forum, and keep invited speakers to five minutes, everyone else to two. In addition, be brief yourself! Mention your goals, such as safety and respect for all. Keep your awareness on large goals, such as the hope that community members get to know the community's various parts. Remember that most communities are not aware of their diversity issues.

5. Awareness work means noticing the weather (the momentary atmosphere reigning in a group); roles (the momentary players, such as "oppressor," "oppressed," "terrorists," "leaders," etc. Each group has its own names for these roles); ghost roles (roles mentioned but not occupied by anyone present); edges (communication breaks); and hot spots (apparently forbidden topics). Be gentle in conveying your awareness; let the people and their processes show you how to proceed. Remember that everyone has *all roles* inside.

6. Suggest an awareness intervention only three times. If it is not picked up, recognize it is not yet "time" for the community as a whole. Take your awareness, then, as a suggestion to yourself. Tell the folks, "Whoops, that's my process, I'll work on it at home."

7. During periods of escalation, try having one speaker at a time discuss the issue. If this does not work, remember the formula for dogs and cats: A in B, and B in A. A little part of B is hearing A, and a little part of A is hearing B, although they may not want to admit it.

E. Consciousness during Attack: Framing and centeredness in conflict

1. A frame helps a picture stand out. Similarly, framing topics, issues, and levels of consciousness ensures clarity. For example, frame the work as being focused either in consensus reality or Dreamland. Talk about oppressors as ghosts if the oppressor

does not see himself or herself as such. *Act out* the oppressors for the forum.

2. If members of a subgroup conflict with each other, frame that conflict by noting how that group is showing all of us how to create community. Take them as a model of diversity.

3. At any one moment, you may want to switch roles and leave the position of the facilitator. Do so consciously and tell others what you are doing.

4. If you get attacked, enter a dialogue with the individual who attacked you, and ask one of your co-workers to facilitate the interaction. This "skirmish" may be helpful for all, especially if your attacker's viewpoint and your viewpoint are two of the central roles in the conflict field—roles that have not yet been sufficiently represented. Being publicly attacked is no fun, but it can eventually benefit everyone.

5. Watch out for clapping, although there is nothing more natural than clapping to show appreciation. However good the clapping may be for the one making the point, the party against whom the point is being made feels ganged up on.

6. Processing problems in a community can be the best way to create immunity to new problems. If moments of togetherness appear, cherish them, for they strengthen the community's immune system.

F. Ending with Why You Began:
Get in touch with the deepest reasons for being

1. Ten minutes before the end of the forum, say, "We have ten minutes left, and we are just beginning to discover various aspects of this organization. What needs to happen next? Who has not spoken? Who will do what? Where and when will we do it?"

2. Don't forget to mention that you are aware of those groups and individuals who have not yet had a chance to speak. This

acknowledgment gives them the chance to speak and ensures that their silence does not turn into vengeance against the group.

3. The central question for you, personally, regarding ending the Open Forum is "Why did you begin?" Why were you interested, what drew you to this job? Mention what the forum did and did not accomplish. What was the great dream that you had around large-group work?

4. Make a statement about participants' evolving knowledge of diversity issues: "Today, we reaffirmed or discovered topics x, y, and z."

5. The linear part of the community wants prescriptions. If you have some, or if the Open Forum produced some, reiterate them. "This is what to do next." Also reiterate any organizational or systemic changes that need to be made. "I notice that systemic (legal, economic) change is needed. Who will work on that?" You might also say, "Let's think about what happened here and how it might apply to workplace ethics."

6. Talk about what you learned, summing things up according to the levels you noticed: "There is work to be done on inner oppression." Or you might say, "How about holding more Open Forums in school (workplace, city)?" Suggest to people that they use an Open Forum format for the next religious or family celebration.

7. Make a list of the community's various groups and Open Forum methods, and support these. Mention that the good things that happened were based in part on their work. Suggest ways they may collaborate with one another in the future. Tell people how to get involved in these groups.

8. Post telephone numbers of people to call in the organization or city for further support (e.g., provide contact numbers for further legal and civil rights help).

9. At the end of the forum, suggest meeting areas in the room to discuss things further, including the hot spots.

10. Announce a possible theme for the second forum; call it something simple, such as "What We Can Do to Make Things

Better." The goal might be to listen more fully about what is really happening and eventually to pose solutions to the issue at hand.

11. You might create a title for a third Open Forum, such as, "What We Have Done So Far and Where We Can Go from Here."

12. Whenever you think about the Open Forum, remember that it is as much an innerwork project as an outer one. It is about You, the community. That is the way to thank the Great Spirit.

PART II.

A Second Revolution:

Use Awareness as Your Main Power Source

A. The Psychosocial Activist:
The community's material and psychological essence

1. More advanced awareness work recognizes that awareness of the Dreaming, of ghosts and hot spots, of innerwork and teamwork is a second revolution, a revolution calling for moment-to-moment awareness. The first revolution is awareness of inequality and the need for equal distributions of material goods and rights.

2. Remember to thank the elders in a community; they help your facilitation to occur.

3. Thank your team. They pick up whatever the whole organization is feeling. Your team may have to work through the same conflicts as the organization itself. So, if the Open Forum problem is split into opposing parts (which it usually is), your team will probably mirror this fragmentation. Teams work best when team members accept their own diversity.

4. There is always a conflict in style between the emotional and the intellectual roles. Framing the situation by explaining that these are different approaches is usually helpful.

5. Activists who carry on a tirade against the bossy, authoritative, and patriarchal government may be unaware that their style is the "government" in the Dreaming.

6. The psychosocial activist conveys, in essence, "The world is me." We need equal distribution of material possessions and the ongoing awareness of what is happening right now, in each moment.

B. The Dreaming Background to Community: How to go from hopelessness to empowerment and freedom

1. Expressions of hopelessness can be hidden vengeance, a reaction against having been publicly downed. Hopelessness may also be due to the impossibility of dealing with generalities about history and power holders not represented in the moment. Represent these entities as ghost roles. Remember that the notion of multinational corporations can be a projection of our own tendency to globalize or generalize, which ignores individuals.

2. The Open Forum is a reaction to all forms of hopelessness about social change. Recall that some hopelessness is really depression due to dealing only with outer realities, with statistics and facts. Don't forget the Dreaming, play, and imagination.

3. There is no choir to preach to; in fact, the forum—and every group—is a conglomeration similar to the world itself.

4. People leave the forum early for a variety of reasons. Yet they have not left entirely, for the role that they "brought" to the forum in the apparent form of their personhood exists independent of them in the form of ghost roles that will always be wherever there are humans. Therefore, let folks come and go as they like.

184

5. In a way, nothing at the Open Forum is personal, though it surely feels personal. What happens is a cosmic drama looking for people to play its roles. When these people are gone, others will most likely take their place.

6. It is common to criticize or denigrate authorities, but remember that the critic who is doing the downing may be an "authority" as well.

7. Chaos and escalation around hot spots are scary, but if you suggest trusting the people in the heat to do their best, if you focus and listen, escalation—and war—become unnecessary.

8. We are our social role, and we are free of all roles. Like everything else in this universe, we are a mixture of stardust, a piece of the infinite, and can therefore be proud of our particular mixture.

9. Even the person who is the most impossible is a role; let's say "the tyrant." You may have to step out of the facilitator role for a moment and confront her yourself, using awareness to point out her unwittingly unconscious use of power. But make sure you don't stay in that role of consciousness-maker, of heroic educator, too long; it belongs to the community's own awakening.

10. If you can't confront the tyrant, perhaps fear is the next ghost role to enact.

C. The Media as Wake-up Dream:
The media is a problem as long as you don't splash

1. The media is to the world as a big dream is to a sleeping person. Both ask you for sound bites and make you feel more important than the rest of your community.

2. Become aware of all viewpoints within yourself instead of being polarized by the media and confronted with the good/bad, success/failure viewpoints.

3. The media take problems out of context. Appreciate the story they are trying to tell, but bring it back into context, reminding everyone of the larger goals and the forum's historical background.

4. Dialogue and subtle feeling changes do not make money. Good and evil are simpler to see than slow, subtle awareness changes and slight immeasurable weather variations in organizations' atmosphere. Yet process is where important, immeasurable changes slowly occur.

5. If you are passive relative to the media, you will see it as evil and yourself as good. However, if you choose to be active, you can use your own dualistic thinking to create your own story.

6. Write out the story of what you imagine could—or should—happen in your organization or city. This is the story that is driving you. Write it out in detail. It is the story that is using you to make it conscious to all.

7. The whole truth includes subtlety and dialogue, as well as the personality and standpoint of the reporter. No one is only a role. Who that reporter is belongs in the story.

8. Did that forum work? Yes, always, in terms of increased awareness. If all it did was to announce and advertise its occurrence, it was a success. Anything else is dessert.

D. The Flu Shot against War:
The sentient essence of retaliation

1. Any single war is world war, since war comes from conflicts no one deals with.

2. War theories do not suggest working with large diverse groups of conflicting contestants, which is the place where conflict finally breaks out.

3. Open Forums can reduce violence by modeling awareness in innerwork, relationship work, rank, and power at all levels and moments.

4. To prevent violence and war in the forum, supplement working on one topic by working with awareness of all topics at the same time. Under the umbrella of one problem lie all the others. While working on race, remember gender. While working on sexism, remember economics. While working on economics, remember dreaming, biology, military theory, etc.

5. Severe conflict challenges us to make everyday life more exciting and to risk processing diversity issues.

6. When in the midst of violence, join the person in an apparently extreme state and say, "YES! I understand where 'we' are coming from," to ameliorate conflict.

7. If you feel into the violence, you will realize that agony cannot dissipate if its essence is not discovered. If it is real for you, take the role of the violent one, saying something like "Please remember that we are not just retaliating, we are searching for equality."

8. Reduce world violence with moment-to-moment awareness of oppression. Potential violence is a rapid path to outer equality and inner freedom. With all this in mind comes the recognition that war is old-fashioned.

9. Near-death experiences in wartime remind us that we are not just the victim or the persecutor. Knowing this might help some of us to learn to switch roles before the end of life forces us to do so.

E. The Open Forum as the Elder's Monastery: The mindlessness that helps the universe dance

1. Elders rise above the troubles of the moment, care for the whole, and experience the world as their family. A particular feature characterizes these people: they have learned to heal themselves from the deep wound of being shamed or stripped of social power.

2. People from marginalized communities know the details of oppression. In the Open Forum they have more spiritual power and, in principle, are better able to facilitate and educate others. Within the context and social setting of Open Forums, such people can change the world.

3. The elder is a mystic in action, a person connected to the suffering of her people, and to something infinite and timeless. She often brings perennial wisdom to bear on the anguish of the moment.

4. After training, do your best as a facilitator. When you are exhausted, forget the facilitator. Let her go. That paradoxical moment allows the elder to arise, and amazing things sometimes happen.

5. From the elder's perspective, the Open Forum, which may seem like hell to the ordinary state of mind, is a monastery. She sees the world as a sacred place where all events are trying to strengthen the sense of a community of all beings.

6. From the spiritual viewpoint, things are easier as a facilitator if you realize that people are in roles that nature asks them to play. In fact, social action needs dreaming to complete itself. Relationships are nature's calligraphy, a dream theater created by nature. Seeing this frees you to assist her in painting the future picture of community.

Endnotes

Preface

1. I discuss the concept of deep democracy in *The Leader as Martial Artist, An Introduction to Deep Democracy*, HarperCollins, 1992, and its sequel, *Sitting in the Fire, Large Group Transformation Using Conflict and Diversity*, Lao Tse Press, 1997. See the bibliography for more.

Chapter 1

1. On December 10, 1948, the General Assembly of the United Nations adopted and proclaimed the Universal Declaration of Human Rights. Following this historic act, the Assembly called on all member countries to publicize the text of the Declaration and "to cause it to be disseminated, displayed, read, and expounded principally in schools and other educational institutions, without distinction based on the political status of countries or territories."

2. See the revised edition: *Robert's Rules of Order Revised*, 1996 (www.ConstitutionSociety.org). Henry Martyn Robert was born in 1837 and died on May 11, 1923, Hormel, N.Y. A graduate (1857) of the U.S. Military Academy, West Point,

N.Y., Robert retired (1901) with the rank of brigadier general. During the Civil War (1861–65), while stationed at New Bedford, he presided over a turbulent meeting of his church; on later investigation, he learned that there was no generally accepted set of parliamentary rules. He then began to write his own code, breaking with the English precedent when necessary, producing the *Pocket Manual of Rules of Order for Deliberative Assemblies* in 1876. The work was immediately successful and went through numerous editions during Robert's lifetime, including the 1915 revision, entitled *Robert's Rules of Order Revised for Deliberative Assemblies* (revised, 1971, as *Robert's Rules of Order Revised*). Robert's *Parliamentary Practice* (1921) and *Parliamentary Law* (1922) were still in print in the 1970s.

3. In the preface to *Robert's Rules of Order Revised* found on the website of the Constitution Society, it said: "The object of Rules of Order is to assist an assembly to accomplish in the best possible manner the work for which it was designed. To do this it is necessary to restrain the individual somewhat, as the right of an individual, in any community, to do what he pleases, is incompatible with the interests of the whole. Where there is no law, but every man does what is right in his own eyes, there is the least of real liberty. . . . It is much more material that there should be a rule to go by than what that rule is; that there may be a uniformity of proceeding in business, not subject to the caprice of the chairman or capriciousness of the members. It is very material that order, decency, and regularity be preserved in a dignified public body."

4. The history of parliamentary process from Anglo-Saxon tribes and their village-moot and "folkmoot" through the creation of Robert's Rules can be found in *Robert's Rules of Order*, newly revised, 1990, 9th Edition by General Henry M. Robert, Harper Collins, NY. According to Robert, "The great lesson for democracies to learn is for the majority to give to the minority a full, free opportunity to present their side of the case, and then for the minority, having failed to win a majority to their view, gracefully to submit and to recognize the action as that of the entire organization, and cheerfully to assist in carrying it out, until they can secure its repeal."

Arnold Mindell, Ph.D.

Chapter 3

1. The original name of this group was the Black Panther Party for Self-Defense, an American Black revolutionary party founded in 1966 in Oakland, California, by Huey Newton and Bobby Seale. The party's original purpose was to patrol Black ghettos to protect residents from acts of police brutality. The Panthers eventually developed into a Marxist revolutionary group that called for the arming of all Blacks, the exemption of Blacks from the draft and from all sanctions of so-called white America, the release of all Blacks from jail, and the payment of compensation to Blacks for centuries of exploitation by white Americans.

Chapter 6

1. Harrison Owen is the originator of Open Space technology and the author of *Open Space Technology: A User's Guide.*

Chapter 8

1. She tried to protect herself, saying, "Wait a minute, I love both." Shortly thereafter, another woman stood up on her sister's side and proudly said, "Listen here, folks, God is neither black or white. And I am first and foremost a child of God!"

Chapter 11

1. See Timothy Conway's wonderful book, *Women of Power and Grace* (New Californian Wake Up Press, 1994). Anasuya Devi was born in 1923 and died around 1996. She did a lot of social action work, was a kind of Mother Teresa in her own way. Some of the things she says are shocking, so hold your breath. When one of her disciples asked her, if the mind impels one to do wrong, isn't that wrong? She answered: "I keep no lists of right and wrong, my child. One fellow came lamenting he had discovered some bad qualities of himself and asked can even these be divine? I told him you wouldn't have those qualities if God didn't want them." When asked what to do about the world, she said; "Do whatever you are impelled to do. For isn't that IT that impels you?" In other words, what seems personal is coming from cosmic energies.

Bibliography

Atlee, Tom. 2001. *The Co-Intelligence Institute Promotes Collaboration.*
    <http://www.co-intelligence.org>.
Boal, Augusto. 1985. *Theatre of the Oppressed.* Translated by Charles
    McBride. New York: Theatre Communications Group.
Bondurant, Joan V. 1965. *Conquest of Violence: The Gandhian
    Philosophy of Conflict,* rev. Berkeley, Calif.: University of
    California Press.
Castaneda, Carlos. 1969. *Journey to Ixtlan.* New York: Simon and
    Schuster.
Constitution Society. *Robert's Rules of Order Revised.*
    <http://www.constitution.org/rror/rror—03.htm>
Conway, Timothy. 1994. *Women of Power and Grace.* Santa Barbara,
    Calif.: New Californian Wake Up Press.
Fisher, Louis, ed. 1962. *The Essential Gandhi.* New York: Vintage Books.
Mandela, Nelson. 1999. *Long Walk to Freedom: The Autobiography of
    Nelson Mandela.* New York: Econo-Clad Books.
Mindell, Arnold. 2000. *Dreaming While Awake: Techniques for 24-
    Hour Lucid Dreaming.* Charlottesville, Va.: Hampton Roads
    Publishing Co.

————. 2000. *Quantum Mind: The Edge between Psychology and Physics*. Portland, Ore.: Lao Tse Press.

————. 1997. *Sitting in the Fire: Large Group Transformation Through Diversity and Conflict*. Portland, Ore.: Lao Tse Press.

———— 1992/2000. *The Leader as Martial Artist, An Introduction to Deep Democracy, Techniques and Strategies for Resolving Conflict and Creating Community*. HarperCollins: San Francisco. Portland, Ore.: Lao Tse Press.

————. 1990. *The Year I: Global Process Work with Planetary Tensions*. New York and London: Penguin-Arkana.

————. 1987. *The Dreambody in Relationships*. New York and London: Penguin.

Owen, Harrison. 1992. *Open Space Technology: A User's Guide*. Potomac, Maryland. Abbott Pub.

Reiss, Gary. 2000. *Changing Ourselves, Changing the World*. Tempe, Ariz.: New Falcon Press.

Robert, Gen. Henry M. 1990. *Robert's Rules of Order Revised*, 9th ed. New York: HarperCollins.

Sharp, Gene. 1973. *Power and Struggle: Politics of Nonviolent Action*. Boston: Porter Sargent.

Tart, Charles. 1989. *Open Mind, Discriminating Mind: Reflections on Human Possibilities*. New York: Harper & Row.

Ury, William L. 1999. *Getting to Peace, Transforming Conflict at Home, at Work, and in the World*. New York: Viking Press.

Washington Post. 23 August, 1999.

Weitzel, Tim, and Gary Had. 2001. Make friends with the wild things. *ASTD* (American Society for Training and Development) *Training & Development Magazine*.

Zeitlin, Aaron. 1940. Warner Brothers for Mills Music, Inc.

Index

About the Author

Arnold Mindell, Ph.D., is the author of fifteen other books including *The Dreammaker's Apprentice* (Hampton Roads, 2001), *Quantum Mind* (Lao Tse Press, 1999), and *The Shaman's Body* (HarperSanFranscico, 1993). He is known throughout the world for his innovative synthesis of dreams and bodywork, Jungian therapy and group process, consciousness, shamanism, quantum physics, and conflict resolution. Dr. Mindell travels widely in the U.S. and abroad, holding workshops and making frequent appearances at professional conferences and on television and radio shows. He lives in Portland, Oregon.